FACEBOOK FAIRYTALES

MODERN-DAY
MIRACLES
to Inspire
THE HUMAN SPIRIT

EMILY LIEBERT

Skyhorse Publishing

Skyhorse Publishing books may be purchased in bulk at special discounts
for sales promotion, corporate gifts, fund-raising, or educational purposes.
Special editions can also be created to specifications. For details, contact
the Special Sales Department, Skyhorse Publishing, 555 Eighth Avenue,
Suite 903, New York, NY 10018 or info@skyhorsepublishing.com.

www.skyhorsepublishing.com

10 9 8 7 6 5 4 3 2 1

Library of Congress Cataloging-in-Publication Data

Liebert, Emily.
Facebook fairytales : modern-day miracles to inspire the human spirit /
Emily Liebert.
p. cm.
ISBN 978-1-60239-943-3 (pbk. : alk. paper)
1. Facebook (Electronic resource) 2. Online social networks. 3.
Information technology--Social aspects. I. Title.
HM742.L45 2010
302.30285--dc22
2009039631

Printed in China
Design by LeAnna Weller Smith

Dedication

For my Pop Pop, Alvin Rickel,
who inspired me to chase my dreams and
to never take "no" for an answer. I love and
miss you. And to his namesake, my sweet son
Jaxsyn Alvin. How did I ever live without you?

CONTENTS

One-on-One with
MARK ZUCKERBERG, FACEBOOK CEO
and Founder

Its population exceeds 350 million.

More than 8 billion minutes are spent on it every day.

Over 2 billion photos are uploaded to it each month.

It's available in seventy languages.

If it were a country, it would be the fourth largest across the globe.*

FACEBOOK *Fairytales*

It's Facebook. And it's conquering the world, one user at a time. But who's the man behind the multibillion-dollar curtain—the wizard of social networking Oz, so to speak? That would be twenty-five-year-old wunderkind, Mark Zuckerberg, who, along with three of his Harvard classmates, launched the site from his college dorm room in 2004. Yes, he was only twenty years old at the time. And, yes, he really is the brains behind the brawn.

So, when I set out to write this book, I knew I had to speak with the wizard himself. How else would I be able to truly capture the essence of Facebook—to dig deep into the zeitgeist of this cultural phenomenon?

He's reticent, I was warned. *He doesn't like interviews with press and agrees to very few. Even his appearance on* The Oprah Winfrey Show *was discussed for more than a year with producers*. The cautionary tales came rolling in.

But—alas—I've never been one to prescribe to the hype. And it's a good thing. As it turned out, Mark was not only excited about the concept for *Facebook Fairytales,* but he was also more than happy to share some of his insights into the site's rampant popularity and unbridled growth.

Born and raised in a suburb of New York City, by his father Edward—a dentist—and his mother Karen, a psychiatrist, Mark received his first computer in sixth grade and was instantly captivated. "Some people like takings things apart and seeing how they work," he explains. "I was more interested in programming and figuring out how to make the computer do new things."

And that's exactly what he did—at first, getting his feet wet with the development of basic communication tools and games. Years later, enrolled at the distinguished preparatory school, Phillips Exeter Academy, Mark began tackling more significant endeavors—building a program to help his father's employees communicate, and developing a music player called Synapse, which utilized artificial intelligence to gauge users' listening habits.

By the time he'd graduated from high school, Mark knew his way around a computer, and, during his sophomore year at Harvard, he conjured a seemingly simple idea: a website where members could connect with friends and family in a private online setting. "I'd messed around with a lot of different things, and Facebook was something that just immediately resonated with a large group of people. So I stuck with it," Mark says matter-of-factly, nonplussed by the cosmic fame eddying around him. "One of the interesting things about my generation is that we were one of the first groups to grow up with the Internet. All of my childhood friends were using this type of software to communicate, to stay in touch, and to plan things. I'm sure that shaped how I think and played a role in my conception of Facebook."

Still, though, no one else has executed the idea in quite the same way or with quite the same finesse as Mark. Not to mention that none of the other social networking sites have realized Facebook's sweeping success—over a whopping 350 million members worldwide. But, why?

FACEBOOK *Fairytales*

"Because everything is so real," says Mark. "There are so many other sites where people share information, but they're not as authentic. Whereas on Facebook, it's all grounded in who you really are. Your profile represents all this information that's really about you, and it changes the whole feel of the site. When you get a message from someone, their picture is right there next to it, and it's a real picture of them as opposed to some icon. That makes it human."

And Mark should know. After all, he uses the site in the same way everyone else does. "It's how I stay in touch. My family is mostly on the East Coast, and I'm in Palo Alto, California, so I don't get to talk to them every day, but I get to see what they're up to through Facebook, which is pretty cool. And it's the same thing with my girlfriend who goes to school in San Francisco. It's a really neat tool to very quickly and very easily see what's going on with all the people around you."

True. But, like I said to Mark, there has to be more to it. "I think another reason Facebook has taken off ahead of some of the other social networking sites is because we've been very focused on constantly making it easier and easier for people to use. Everyone wants to stay connected with the people they care about, share the stuff they want to share, and control the information so that only the people who they want to see it can actually see it, but not everyone loves using a computer or is really computer-savvy. It's been our goal over the last two years to facilitate the simplest ways of doing these things, and it's obviously caught on."

That would be an understatement. Not only has Facebook "caught on," but it's also garnered unprecedented media attention on a daily basis—from the *New York Times* and the *Wall Street Journal* to *60 Minutes*, *The Today Show*, and, yes, *Oprah*, to name a few. *Time* magazine even named Mark one of "The World's Most Influential People of 2008"—a remarkable distinction for anyone, in particular a twenty-five-year-old Ivy League dropout.

How is Mark managing the overwhelming attention? Like everything else, he's taking it in stride. "Honestly, what matters most to me is the impact of what we're doing—seeing how many people are using Facebook and how many businesses are changing as a result of our progress," he asserts, pausing to contemplate further. "I'm primarily focused on building things. That's what makes me excited. Appearing on TV is not something I concentrate on. We're trying to build a company here. That's what we care about more than what the media is saying about us."

Of course Mark is quick to point out that he takes great pleasure in being approached by common folk—those without a microphone and television camera in tow—and hearing their amazing Facebook stories. "Recently I was in New York, checking into my hotel, and the gentleman who was checking me in had just recently moved to the U.S. from Vietnam," Mark recalls, with a buoyant lilt to his voice. "He told me that all of his friends in Vietnam were on Facebook, and that he'd joined when he came here as a way to stay in touch with them. It's really interesting to hear those kinds of stories, because Facebook was born here in the U.S., but people are using it to maintain correspondence with people half the world away."

That they are. But, what's next—beyond the vast web of connections? Where will Facebook be in five to ten years?

"Facebook is the type of product, like e-mail or like a Web browser, which I expect to become completely ubiquitous. What does the world look like when a billion people are using social networks and they can share even more than they're able to today? A lot more things will be possible. It will change how businesses communicate with their customers, how governments function and communicate with their citizens. As well as, most importantly, how people communicate with their friends and family. We think that 300 million is good progress, but—without a doubt—it's closer to the beginning than the end."

Even better, Mark plans to remain at the helm of his Silicon Valley–based start-up. "I believe that companies and products are best guided by the person who sets the original vision for where they should end up. I would hope that I'm doing this for as long as it's possible."

So do we, Mark.

* Statistics from November 2009.

Introduction

When, nearly two years ago, one of my closest friends from childhood suggested I join a social networking site called Facebook, I was instantly skeptical. For one, I've never been particularly adept at anything technical (translation: I still own a big yellow Walkman).

And besides, the last thing I needed was another distraction from my writing.

About a month later, she nudged again. I'd been urging her to send photos of her two precious babies, and when I pressed her for the umpteenth time, she taunted, "If you join Facebook, you'll be able to see all the photos you'd like." I couldn't resist. I remember thinking, *I'll just join so I can see her photos, but I won't devote any other time to it.* After all, the term "social networking" was new to my vocabulary.

Still, desperate for a photo fix and figuring I'd never get my very persistent friend off my back, I signed up. A few clicks later and I was mesmerized. Not only were loads of people I knew—from past and present—already members, but I felt like I'd been let in on the greatest secret of all time. You see, I've always been a bit of a voyeur. As the editor in chief of a luxury lifestyle magazine for five years, I spent countless hours scouring wedding snapshots and party pics, and I never tired of it. "You really don't need to look at *all* of them," brides would insist, handing over their one thousand photos. And I would dutifully reply, "It's okay; it's my job." What I was actually thinking was, *Hand 'em over; I'm dying for a sneak peek into your life!*

So, when my introduction to Facebook came to be, I felt as though someone out there had designed a site specifically with me in mind. I've since found out that upwards of 350 million people feel exactly the same way!

Introduction

For those of you hiding under a rock, Facebook was founded in 2004 by Harvard student Mark Zuckerberg and his roommates, and is a social utility vehicle for communicating and reconnecting with friends, family, and coworkers. Not only has Facebook become a household staple, but it's also one of the first social networking sites to span generations—from high school and college students to their parents and even grandparents. I can proudly say that three generations of my family are members, and I'm far from alone.

Brad Stone's March 28, 2009, *New York Times* article, "Is Facebook Growing Up Too Fast?" may have said it best: "Facebook promises to change how we communicate . . . by digitally mapping and linking peripatetic people across space and time, allowing them to publicly share myriad and often very personal elements of their lives." The piece also pointed out that "Facebook is rapidly becoming the Web's dominant social ecosystem and an essential personal and business networking tool in much of the wired world."

This got me thinking: Okay, so Facebook is connecting millions of people across the world. It's being used for personal enjoyment and also toward professional growth. But what comes of these millions of connections? There must be some amazing stories, I reasoned—something beyond old friends reuniting. There must be romances, business coups, perhaps even everyday miracles to inspire the human spirit.

That's when my search began. It was also when the concept for this book was born. As someone who's always been fond of telling stories, I felt certain that I could amass a collection of heartwarming, stimulating, and motivational tales that had resulted from these "kismet connections," and that they would emphasize the real-life characters' personal struggles and feats. And I was right. In fact, I was so overwhelmed by the vast selection that it was hard to pick only twenty-five!

From reignited romances, organ donations, and families reunited to business accomplishments, adoptions, and a teenager's life saved, my hope is that readers will relate to these triumphant tales and be charmed by that little spark of magic that sets them apart from your everyday success stories. And, further, I hope that people will appreciate the many different ways Facebook had a hand in these achievements—whether it was through connecting, sharing, updating, communicating, placing an ad, promoting a product, joining a group or cause, or simply by using it as an alternate form of e-mail when a T1 line was struck by lightning (it may sound far-fetched, but it happened to me!).

Facebook is not only a social networking site—it's a cultural revolution. It's opened up an international dialogue, allowing members to connect in the most technologically advanced way. But, more than that, it's truly become the modern-day word of mouth, and the outcome, in the short span of six years, has been an intricate web of connections, the results of which have transformed people's lives in ways they never imagined possible.

Take time reading these stories. If my prediction is correct, they'll rouse you to go that extra mile, to treat others as you'd like to be treated, and to reach for the stars. It's so easy to get wrapped up in the daily grind and to forget that the resilience of the human spirit is truly powerful. My hope is that all of these stories will be savored and will open the hearts of those who relive them through the pages of this book.

Here's hoping *Facebook Fairytales* is the next great Facebook success story. Enjoy!

DONOR *Destiny*

$\mathcal{I}$t was a scorching July day in Tallahassee, Florida, when Cathy Schroeder's best friend from childhood came to visit. But the extreme heat didn't stop the two ladies from sitting on Cathy's front porch, chitchatting about their impending twenty-year high school reunion.

"Who do you think is going to show up?" Cathy speculated.

"Do you think they'll look the same?" her friend indulged.

"What are we going to wear!?" They laughed heartily.

A few days later, back at home, Cathy's friend forwarded her a link to a Facebook page set up to organize the particulars of their reunion. Cathy knew of Facebook—she'd even considered becoming a member—so she joined without delay. By that afternoon, she'd already connected with tons of old friends, one of whom was her ex-boyfriend, Scott Harris. They'd communicated intermittently since college, but Cathy was pleased to have this new forum through which to keep up with him.

Scott reported that he was living in New York with his wife and three daughters. Cathy replied that she and her husband Drew, a firefighter, were the proud parents of their beautiful four-year-old daughter, Olivia. Life was good for both of them.

The following morning, sitting at work and getting little done, Cathy coiled a section of her blonde corkscrew curls around one finger and focused her clear blue eyes on the four sterile walls surrounding her. She'd decorated her office with an array of trinkets and artwork from her husband and daughter, but even her Mardi Gras decor wasn't enough to brighten the barren backdrop of the government building in which she worked. She decided to break the monotony by logging on to Facebook, and, as she idly scanned through her friends' status updates, one in particular caught her eye. It was from Scott, and it read:

I have a friend named Beth who needs a kidney donor. If you have type-O blood, please visit her website.

Cathy swallowed deliberately. She was type O; she knew as much from regularly donating blood over the years. She'd never considered being an organ donor, though, and that didn't change when she read Scott's post. After all, this woman was a complete stranger.

But, still, Cathy was intrigued and wanted to learn more. This clearly meant a lot to Scott, she told herself, and that was enough.

Cathy promptly logged on to Beth's site—kidney4beth .com—and was confronted with a story too heart-wrenching to digest: Over a thousand miles away in Scarsdale, New York, a thirty-three-year-old mother of two named Beth Abramowitz was fighting kidney disease with only one kidney, functioning at 10 percent. She was in desperate need of a donor, and time was running out.

Completely devastated, Cathy's mind started racing. *How would Beth's young children move on if she died? What if she didn't get to watch them learn to ride a bike?*

Or go to the prom? Or walk down the aisle?! Cathy knew that every minute of every day was beyond precious to this woman, and something inside of her couldn't let it go. Even if she couldn't save Beth's life, she had to at least reach out.

On August 5, 2008, Cathy did just that. She wrote one brief message that, unbeknownst to her, would be the catalyst for an elaborate progression of life-changing events:

Beth:

I'm sure this is going to sound odd—heck, it sounds odd to me—but I wanted to reach out to you. I know Scott Harris and recently linked up with him via Facebook. I saw his post about you, checked out your website, messaged Scott, Googled transplants, ignored most of my work this morning, and here I am.

Have you found a donor? I'm so sorry you're sick. I can't imagine, especially as a mommy. Please write me if you'd like.

Cathy

That afternoon, Cathy returned from a meeting to find a reply from Beth in her in-box:

Hi Cathy,

Thank you for contacting me. We have not found a donor. Could you please forward my website to any family and friends?

Thank you so much!

Beth

And by that evening, Cathy was responding with a message that even she could barely wrap her head around:

Beth,

I would like more information about what is involved . . . testing, surgery, recovery, etc. I am O+, and strangely enough, thinking about this.

I'm not a wacko, and I can't guarantee it would work, but I would like to learn more.

Maybe you could recommend some websites for me to check out . . . I understand if this is weird.

Cathy

Over the course of the next few weeks, Cathy learned more and more about Beth's condition from her newfound friend, and by scouring the Web for information. She couldn't explain why, not even to herself, but she still couldn't let it go. She thought, *If I can help this woman, that would be the most wonderful blessing.* And when they discovered that they both had daughters named Olivia, Cathy couldn't shake the feeling that their connection was meant to be.

For Beth's part, she was cautiously optimistic. She'd been contacted by so many people and led down so many dead ends. But this woman, Cathy, sounded so intelligent and kind that she couldn't help but get her hopes up.

Only, one minor obstacle remained: Cathy hadn't told her husband, Drew, and she struggled with the heavy task at hand. How do you tell the person closest to you that you want to donate one of your organs to a woman you don't know, over a thousand miles away? What would Drew think? What *could* he think? Cathy was terrified he'd say she'd gone mad!

And she was right. When Cathy finally mustered up the courage to divulge her intentions, Drew was confused, to say the least.

"This is nuts!" he exclaimed, panic suffusing his face. "What's missing here?" he questioned feverishly. "This is coming out of nowhere. This isn't a family member or a friend you've known forever!" He stared at her, baffled by the information he'd just received.

"You're a fireman; you risk your life all the time for people you don't know. What makes this any different?" Cathy countered coolly.

"There's a vast difference between doing something you've gone through years of training for, where you understand the hazards," he insisted. "I may take risks, but they're controlled risks, and I know how to be safe. You want to let someone put you under, dig around inside your body, remove an organ, sew you up, and say, 'Have a nice day!'"

"This is something I just have to do." Cathy was adamant. "I need to at least try and help."

Drew knew better than to dispute that. When Cathy set her mind on something, there was no changing it. And despite his fears and concerns, he knew he could either support her or not, and that the latter wasn't going to get him anywhere. If Drew was being honest with himself, while it was certainly out of the blue, it didn't really surprise him that Cathy wanted to do something nice for someone. Cathy had to give of herself to exist. She always had to be out there shaking the tree, searching for that next thing that was going to change the world or make her feel better about living on the planet. Whereas most people were only involved with what was two feet in front of their nose, generosity came naturally to Cathy. How could he deny her that?

In the meantime, back in New York, Beth was becoming increasingly optimistic. *Was this woman really willing to get tested?* She seemed to understand the extensive pain and anguish that the process would inevitably entail. Twelve people had been denied already, having failed the vigorous health-screening exams. Beth's prospects were dwindling, and, studying her list of crossed-out names, she realized that there was only one left—Cathy's.

Throughout the following weeks, Cathy and Beth's relationship blossomed as Cathy took preliminary blood tests and helped Drew process what she was determined to do. She knew he wasn't happy about her decision, but he'd promised to support her, and that was all she needed. Cathy felt truly blessed that there was even a possibility she could help someone in this amazing way, and went so far as to tell Beth one night on the phone, "Even if I'm not a match, I'm willing to donate one of my kidneys to someone who is, so they can donate to you, thereby creating a chain."

But first Cathy had to explain the situation to her four-year-old daughter, Olivia. Driving home from preschool one afternoon, Cathy broached the subject carefully.

"There's a mommy that lives in New York who's really sick," she said, studying Olivia's face intently. "And I have the opportunity to share a part of my body with her that could make her better."

"What part of your body do you have to share?" Olivia inquired.

"One of my kidneys."

"How many kidneys do you have?"

"Two. But I don't need both of them. And this mommy needs my help."

"Do I have to share mine?"

"No, sweetheart; you don't. But I want you to understand how important this is to me, and that everything is going to be okay. This mommy needs my help so she can be healthy for her children. Her daughter even has the same name as you."

Olivia smiled in silent understanding.

By the end of September, Cathy was making her way to New York to undergo a battery of tests, and to meet Beth and her family for the first time, in hopes that her "what-if" would become a real-life success.

After months of getting to know each other, Cathy was eager to finally see Beth face-to-face, but when she arrived at brunch on Sunday morning and found Beth, her husband Josh, and their daughter Olivia waiting, the inherent awkwardness of the scenario hit her. With her luggage by her side, Cathy embraced Beth uneasily as she searched her mind for a way to ease the tension.

"I want you to know that I believe this is going to work," Cathy said with conviction. "I have no second thoughts."

It wasn't until the following day, however, during a two-hour window between tests, that Cathy and Beth had a chance to sit in Central Park together and solidify their connection. Beth still couldn't believe that this virtual stranger was willing to help her in such a profound way. Cathy was unlike anyone she'd ever known. *Was it plausible that, through all of the miserable testing, this woman was actually thanking* her *for letting her be a part of the experience? Was Cathy for real?* Beth pondered. She seemed more like a guardian angel. But yet, here she was, desperate to do the right thing, and that was all that mattered. This was meant to be, the new friends agreed. Cathy was going to save Beth's life.

A grueling two days later, back in Florida, Cathy finally received the call with her results. It appeared that Cathy had a virus, the transplant coordinator told her—a virus that would make her ineligible to donate a kidney.

Cathy and Beth were crestfallen. All of the desperation Beth had been enduring for two years came crashing down on her, and what remained was a feeling of complete hopelessness. Cathy was the thirteenth person that wasn't going to work out, and Beth was forced to come to terms with the fact that she might die.

But the transplant coordinator wasn't quite satisfied. Based on Cathy's other tests, she simply wasn't convinced that Cathy actually had the virus. They should test again, she told Cathy. The coordinator warned that she might be wrong, but it was worth a shot.

For Cathy, having to wait another two days for the second round of results felt like an impossible task. But Beth told her not to worry. "I have a gold medal in waiting," she said. "We'll get through this."

DONOR Destiny

By the second week in October, after daily calls to the lab, Cathy got her answer. She didn't have the virus. She was a donor match! Leaving work for her lunch break, Cathy called Beth and, together, they screamed and cried tears of happiness, relief, and fear. The week before Thanksgiving, it was decided: Cathy would head back to New York to give Beth a part of herself. And nothing could have made her happier.

On the eve of the surgery—just over three months after Cathy's initial message to Beth—both families, including Beth's parents, gathered for an intensely emotional dinner to celebrate the future and to embark on their incredible journey together.

As the meal came to a close, Beth's mother, an antique jewelry collector, presented Cathy with a very special gift—a necklace made of marble-sized crystals. Her note read:

The Japanese believe that crystals have a strong healing power as long as they've been unharmed. All of the crystals on this necklace are wound together, but still intact.

It was her parting good luck charm.

The following morning, as Cathy was wheeled into the operating room at New York Presbyterian, her daughter, Olivia, squeezed her hand tenderly and said, "I love you, Mommy. I know everything is going to be okay."

And that it is. The surgery was a success.

Over a thousand miles away once more, Beth and Cathy still speak often and are savoring their happy, healthy lives with friends and family around them.

"It's amazing that one post on Facebook could bring two complete strangers from different parts of the country together, and that the end result could be life-saving," Beth muses. "When I think about Cathy, it brings me to tears every time. I mean, how do you thank someone for allowing you to watch your children grow up?"

TWO

WAITING FOR *Baby*

t was only three weeks after Melissa Segal had moved to Washington, D.C., in August 2001, that she met Seth Edlavitch at a barbecue for a local volunteer organization. Four years later they were married. And shortly after that, the couple began pursuing their mutual dream of starting a family.

Given that they were in their mid-thirties, Melissa and Seth made the decision early on to try to conceive naturally, but agreed that if it wasn't working after a few months, they'd seek out a fertility specialist. Melissa's proverbial biological clock was ticking, and since they wanted more than one child, they knew time was of the essence.

Six months passed, with Melissa tracking her ovulation cycle religiously, but the outcome was never positive.

"It'll be fine," Seth assured her. "It'll happen for us eventually."

But Melissa wasn't convinced. "Every time it doesn't work, I'm devastated," she explained. "And I don't want to continue to endure the disappointment month after month."

Seth understood. After all, he acknowledged, it wasn't his body.

So, in January 2006, eager to expedite the process, Melissa made a call to the fertility center. And, after a thorough evaluation, the couple was told that while Melissa's tests were all normal, there was an issue on Seth's end, making in vitro fertilization (IVF) their only feasible option.

Melissa and Seth were undaunted. Their goal was to become pregnant, and even though it meant a succession of procedures and shots for Melissa, often administered by Seth, they were ready to tackle the process together.

Fortunately, everything went smoothly. Melissa stimulated above average from the hormones, fourteen eggs were retrieved, five of them fertilized into perfect embryos, and two were transferred into Melissa's uterus. All they had to do was wait a couple of weeks for the good news.

About two weeks after the transfer, the call came in from the nurse at their doctor's office. Melissa, a teacher, sat at the front desk at her school, with the landline on speaker and Seth on her cell phone.

"Congratulations! You're going to be parents!" the nurse announced.

Everything was finally coming together for Seth and Melissa.

Over the course of the following weeks, all of Melissa's tests indicated normal progress, and when it was finally time for the ultrasound, they were both beyond excited. As Melissa lay on the examining table, the doctor probed her stomach.

"There are two heartbeats," he said. But then he cautioned, "One is strong and the other is faint. Chances are you'll have one healthy baby."

How could they argue with that? One healthy baby was all they'd wanted.

Another week passed, and Melissa and Seth headed back to the doctor for ultrasound number two. This time, as the doctor leaned in to look at the screen, his eyes widened and he whispered something inaudible to the technician. Melissa and Seth's hearts raced in unison. Was there something wrong with the baby?

"Wow! You're having identical twins," the doctor declared. "And there is still another heartbeat there, as well." *Three babies!*

"There better not be four the next time we come in," Seth joked, though he was confounded more than anything. Two he could handle. Three at one time—he wasn't so sure.

But by the third ultrasound, the other embryo had reabsorbed, and Seth and Melissa were simply thrilled to be carrying identical twins with strong, healthy heartbeats. Life was good.

And it continued to be good, despite some routine bleeding and a trip to the emergency room, which confirmed that not only were the twins doing well, but that Melissa was carrying two boys!

At twenty weeks, Melissa was waddling around her classroom—measuring, looking, and feeling seven months along—unaccustomed to any extra weight on her five-foot-two frame. It was a Tuesday, and, just like any other day, she made her way around the room, tidying up after her students. As she continued her cleaning, suddenly there was pain—intense pain in her stomach and back, followed by a trip to the doctor.

"The heartbeats are fine," he confirmed. "Your back probably hurts because you're so big."

Melissa breathed a sigh of relief.

Two days later, though, she had another scare when her mucus plug came out.

"Normal," the doctor reassured via telephone. "If you want to come in, you can, although there's nothing to be worried about."

But Melissa wasn't taking any chances, and on Friday of that week—to set her mind at ease for the upcoming weekend—she visited the doctor's office once again to make sure everything was still moving along as planned.

"The heartbeats sound good," the physician on call encouraged her. "Let me just do a quick internal exam, and then you'll be on your way."

As Melissa waited, pleased to be doing anything positive for her babies-to-be, she let her mind wander to the happy times she and Seth would spend with their two sons. But her daydream was quickly interrupted.

"Crap," the doctor said, as a dark shadow cast over his face. "You're two centimeters dilated and eighty to ninety percent effaced. You are in labor. You have to go right to the hospital."

In a panic, Melissa called Seth. He was an hour away and it was raining heavily outside. Melissa's friend would have to pick her up and take her to the hospital, they decided, and Seth would meet them there.

At the hospital, medicine was immediately administered to stop Melissa's contractions, but it was too late. She was going into premature labor and the babies would not survive.

"How are you going to get them out?" Melissa cried, overwhelmed with alarm.

"You're going to have to deliver them," the nurse told her. "I'm so sorry."

Besieged by fear and in a haze of confusion and sorrow, Melissa had no choice but to deliver two beautiful baby boys, whose lungs were not developed enough for them to live.

And by three-thirty in the morning, it was finally over. Exhausted and grief-stricken, Melissa was wheeled to her room, where Seth climbed into bed with her so they could finally cry together, alone at last.

Holding Melissa in his arms, Seth said, "This was horrible, but we're going to get through this. In a year from now you will be pregnant again."

It was the end of their pregnancy, but not the end of their desire for a family.

With Melissa's uterus 80 percent scarred, they knew they had a tough battle ahead, but they weren't intimidated. And exactly one year after their initial IVF cycle, they started the process again.

For some reason, though, Melissa no longer responded to the hormones, and it took three attempts to get just two good embryos, which they transferred. The unfortunate result was a chemical pregnancy—essentially a false positive. They tried one more time, to no avail.

Perhaps it's my body, Melissa reasoned. And so they decided to take a nontraditional route. Melissa's sister, a physician, offered to be their surrogate and carry the baby for them. It wasn't your run-of-the-mill approach, they knew, but Seth and Melissa were willing to try just about anything. Melissa's sister would be implanted, as would Melissa. It was a possibility that they could be carrying Melissa and Seth's children at the very same time.

But disappointment reared its ugly head again when it didn't work for either of them. And one more go of it—with Melissa's sister as the sole carrier—didn't produce either.

It was the summer of 2008. Seth and Melissa had ridden a two-year-long roller coaster with nothing to show for it, and their spirits were down.

"All I want is to be pregnant," Melissa told Seth repeatedly.

"What you really want is to start a family," he pointed out. Melissa agreed with Seth, and they mutually decided to explore adoption.

Neither of them knew much about it, but they were focused on doing something, anything, to make their dream of having a baby come true. So they attended a seminar, researched independent versus agency adoption, and settled on pursuing a combination of both—placing ads and sending applications to two agencies they felt comfortable with.

By August of 2008, Seth and Melissa were home study–approved, and spreading the word to everyone they knew. They created a blog with a short blurb about who they were and what their life was like, and sent it around to friends and family. Seth also created a flyer that Melissa passed along to her colleagues at school and posted at their synagogue. And, while they got lovely responses—others sharing their similar experiences—there weren't any leads on adopting a baby.

Shortly after the Thanksgiving holiday, Seth was tooling around on the computer late one night when a lightbulb went off: *What if I post the flyer on Facebook?* Seth had been a member for a few months and was slowly building connections. He'd heard of the social networking site's viral effect, and decided it certainly couldn't hurt. But he also knew it wasn't possible to post documents on Facebook, so he expertly converted the file to a PDF and then a JPEG, so he could save it as a picture.

"I put our adoption flyer up on Facebook," he informed Melissa the following day.

"Great!" she replied. "The more people who know we're looking, the better."

Two days later, Seth's friend, John, asked if he could post the flyer to his page.

And, in early December, Seth received a call from John's friend, Jenny, a woman from high school who he hadn't spoken to in twenty years. She explained that she had a construction company nearby, and that Lisa, the wife of one of her employees, was eight or nine months pregnant. They already had three kids, and she knew they didn't have a plan for the baby.

Seth Edlavitch **Posted a link**

ADOPTION

Loving, professional couple looking to adopt an infant domestically in the U.S. We are Home Study approved and willing to pay all allowable expenses.

MELISSA

I have been teaching 4th grade for more than 11 years. I am extremely dedicated to teaching and just love working with children. I have always wanted to be a parent, and can't wait to start a family of our own.

I also have an undying commitment to Chloe, my 17 year old cat. I love her and would do anything for her!

SETH

I have spent my whole career working in Public Health. I am currently working with seniors on a Medicare project and really enjoy helping them solve their problems. I also volunteer on Tuesday nights with senior citizens at a local senior home. I am looking forward to sharing my caring and passionate personality with a child.

MELISSA AND SETH

We cannot wait to share our lives with a child. We value family, education, and creating a home of love and respect. We also love to laugh, have fun and enjoy all the things our area has to offer. Please feel free to call or email us at any time.

http://melissaandsethadoption.blogspot.com/

A few days later, Jenny called Seth at work. She said, "Lisa would like to talk to you, but she's too nervous to call. Could you call her?"

"Absolutely!" Seth said, trying not to set his hopes too high.

And that night, beset with frenetic anticipation, Melissa and Seth called Lisa—the woman who could possibly make their dreams come true.

"I'm really nervous," Melissa started.

"So am I," Lisa replied.

Melissa and Seth then told Lisa everything she needed to know about them, and the three decided to meet the following afternoon at a little Starbucks in the Giant supermarket near Lisa's work.

It had been a sleepless night for Melissa and Seth, who sat chatting nervously the next day, awaiting Lisa's arrival. She was right on time, and after awkward introductions and small talk about their shared obsession with *Top Chef*, serious discussions began. They covered Lisa's health habits, family medical history, and her reason for placing the child for adoption—for financial reasons, and the fact that Lisa and her husband weren't prepared to start over with a fourth baby. Lisa even showed Melissa and Seth pictures of her three kids, who were happy and healthy.

When they were finally ready to part ways, Melissa said, "It was so wonderful to meet you. Seth and I definitely want to talk about things. I'm sure you and your husband do as well." And then she asked nervously, "Would it be possible for us to call you tomorrow?"

"You can call me later tonight, if you'd like," Lisa offered, smiling warmly.

Melissa and Seth smiled back. Something just felt right about this woman.

When they spoke later that evening, it was decided. Both parties wanted to move forward. In a matter of weeks, Melissa and Seth would have a brand-new baby!

And on December 30, 2008, the day before Seth's birthday, Noah Benjamin was welcomed into the world, with Melissa and Seth in the delivery room by Lisa and her husband's side. Two days later, on January 1, Seth and Melissa finally brought their baby home.

"It was so poetic starting the New Year with our new son," Melissa reflects. "Noah means 'rest,' and we feel like after this long journey, we can finally do just that."

STATUS *Update*

*S*arah Brysk and Michael Cohen were smitten. As smitten as two teenagers could be, that is, after meeting at a winter seminar in 1990, for their national youth group camp.

Sarah—a La Jolla, California, girl—was sixteen. Michael, an "older man" at nineteen, hailed from Yardley, Pennsylvania, a small community in Bucks County bordered by the Delaware River, and not far from the site of their fleeting romance.

But, after working together as counselors the following summer, Sarah and Michael fell out of touch. And, despite the fact that their older brothers were friends by virtue of attending the same camp, they never received an update as to the other one's whereabouts or goings-on.

Fast-forward fifteen years. Michael, an acclaimed political speechwriter—who had been in a handful of long-term relationships—was residing in the Murray Hill section of Manhattan. Sarah had moved to San Diego, married a man she'd grown up with, and had then relocated to New York, where she was employed as a social worker at NYU—her bus stop just steps from Michael's apartment.

For two years, Sarah and Michael traversed the same neighborhood but never once crossed paths. They simply went about their daily lives, oblivious to each other's close proximity, until 2007, when Sarah and her husband abandoned the Big Apple for Seattle.

Unlike most newlyweds, though, the thrill of starting a new life together in a new city wasn't enough for Sarah. It wasn't enough to silence the voice inside her, urging—even beseeching—her to get out of her troubled marriage.

And in July of 2008, that's exactly what she did. With the support of friends and family, Sarah packed up her belongings and moved back to San Diego to be closer to her parents and to spend the summer traveling and regrouping before plotting her future. She'd need to find a job and a place to live, she knew, but, on the heels of her separation, what she desired most was some time to breathe the fresh air of freedom.

A few weeks later, visiting her longtime friend Katie in New Mexico, the two women sat in Katie's home office, catching up and gossiping about this or that, when Katie broached the subject of Facebook, hoping to coax Sarah into an impromptu tutorial.

"I haven't joined yet, but I really want to try it," Katie hinted. "How about showing me the ropes?"

Sarah, who'd become a member of the social networking site the previous winter, hadn't devoted much time to it. After all, she'd been far too focused on enduring and finally escaping her increasingly problematic relationship. But, now, Sarah was finally in a place where she could reconnect with old friends, relieved not to have to explain her transient marriage.

"Let's do it!" Sarah said, walking Katie through each step on an adjacent computer.

As her friend progressed, Sarah continued to detail different features. "See this alumni group?" Sarah motioned to her screen. "This is for people who went to my summer camp. I'm going to join so I can find some of my old friends."

Katie watched intently.

"I know that guy!" Sarah pointed to the computer again. "So I'm going to connect with him. And, I can also see who else he's friends with." Katie nodded as Sarah scanned through his list. "Oh my God! There's Michael Cohen. I totally made out with him!" Sarah laughed.

"You have to reach out. Maybe he's single!" Katie smiled roguishly.

Sarah took her friend's advice and, before long, Michael had accepted her friend request.

A couple of days passed, and, still in Santa Fe, Sarah logged on to Facebook again. Noticing Michael was also logged on, she tried to say hello via Facebook's chat feature. But Michael, inundated with professional commitments, was too busy to acknowledge her affable attempt.

Undeterred, Sarah tried to connect via chat a few more times. But—still—Michael was unresponsive. And, finally, by the end of August, feeling unnecessarily rejected, Sarah sent Michael a direct message on Facebook, simple and to the point, in the event that he was truly intent on disregarding her.

Hey!
How are you?
Would love to know what you're up to these days!

This time Michael responded, reporting that he was living in Brooklyn and working as a Senior Fellow at the New America Foundation.

Sarah hastily looked him up online and was seriously impressed by what she uncovered. Not only was the photo of Michael on his website really cute, but his bio read like an encyclopedia of accomplishments. Beyond his day job, he'd authored a book, titled *Live from the Campaign Trail: The Greatest Presidential Campaign Speeches of the Twentieth Century and How They Shaped Modern America*. Michael was also, it read, a frequent commentator on politics and international affairs for the *Wall Street Journal*, the *New York Times*, and the *Washington Post*, among other preeminent publications. And, as if all that wasn't remarkable enough, he'd previously served in the U.S. Department of State as chief speechwriter for U.S. Representative to the United Nations, Bill Richardson, and Undersecretary of State, Stuart Eizenstat.

Wow! Sarah mused, taking it all in.

At first, they stuck to sharing old camp stories, but before long, an intense message correspondence ensued. They filled each other in on their respective lives and even flirted a little. Michael, it turned out, had recently ended a yearlong relationship.

With this knowledge in hand, Sarah casually mentioned her upcoming trip out East: "My mom and I will be heading your way in a couple of weeks, to visit my aunt and 102-year-old grandmother," she wrote. "If you're around, I'd love to see you."

Michael replied that he would be around, and was all for a reunion.

FACEBOOK *Fairytales*

Oh my God! I'm going to see Michael Cohen again, after all these years. Sarah's mind raced with the possibilities.

Michael, on the other hand, was intrigued, but maintained his skeptical posture about romance in general. It simply wasn't his style to get overly excited about anything until it was a reality.

Nonetheless, in early September, Sarah prepared for her trip to New York, by which time she and Michael had chatted extensively via Facebook. There was something about the bulk of their connection having been in writing that Sarah delighted in. It was reminiscent of an old-fashioned romance, only with an obvious modern twist.

I wonder if there could actually be something between us, Sarah ruminated, despite Michael's romantic reticence. She had no idea if his feelings matched hers, but one thing was clear: their get-together was unlikely to be purely platonic.

On September 9, at 4 P.M., Sarah's plane landed at John F. Kennedy International Airport, and that night, she took a taxicab to Brooklyn to meet Michael at the General Greene restaurant—a New York hot spot.

Walking through the front door, Sarah spotted Michael at the bar and felt an instant spark. Michael, too, liked what he saw, but—as usual—didn't allow himself to think much beyond their dinner date.

Hours later, though, his mind-set was beginning to change. And the reunited lovebirds spent not only the following day together, but a large chunk of Sarah's week in New York, engaging in all manner of amorous activities—

with Sarah's mother, aunt, and grandmother encouraging their interactions wholeheartedly.

Still, Sarah wasn't sure if Michael was looking merely for a fun-filled week or something more until her final day in Manhattan, when he dropped her off, via Vespa, at her aunt's Upper East Side apartment and handed her an inscribed copy of his book. The touching dedication referenced his chapter on William Jennings Bryan—the 41st United States Secretary of State under President Woodrow Wilson, and one of the most admired speakers in American history, renowned for his imposing voice.

For Michael, it was the most important speech in the book.

Reluctant to leave, Sarah returned to San Diego, and Michael immediately made plans to visit two weeks later, during the third week in September. They had brunch with Sarah's family, who adored her new beau.

The following night over dinner, Michael's eyes welled with tears as he confessed to Sarah, "I've fallen in love with you." Fortunately, the feeling was mutual. And what resulted was a whirlwind of subsequent visits. First, Michael returned to California in October and met all of her dearest friends. Then Sarah flew to New York and accompanied Michael to Pennsylvania, where she was introduced to his parents. Next came Washington, D.C., for the presidential election, and—finally—Michael traveled to California for the last time over the Thanksgiving holiday to help Sarah pack up her things so she could move to Brooklyn, where they would cohabit full-time.

On December 2, Michael, Sarah, and her two English bulldogs set out for New York to commence their new lives—together.

Two months passed, and by February, everything was going better than expected. Sarah was asleep in bed, waiting for Michael to arrive home from a business trip, when—at one-thirty in the morning—he shook her awake.

"I've been thinking about it, and we should get married. I don't want to wait."

"Okay," Sarah replied groggily, resting her head on her pillow and nodding off. She must have been dreaming.

Or not. The next morning, Michael prompted her: "Do you remember our conversation from last night?" She did.

"Yes! Let's get married!" she said. "We can go to City Hall and invite just our parents."

"Really? Wouldn't you rather have a traditional ceremony and reception?" Michael asked, reversing their typical roles.

They debated the pros and cons and, eventually, devised a scheme.

They'd invite Sarah's parents to New York in early March for a long weekend, under the auspices of meeting Michael's parents. It would be an indication that things were getting more serious, but they'd have no idea that during said trip Michael and Sarah would become husband and wife.

With their plan set in motion, the conspiring couple eagerly awaited the big reveal. On the Tuesday night prior to Sarah's parents' arrival, they planned to have a casual dinner with friends at their old haunt, the General Greene. Unbeknownst to Sarah, however, their casual dinner with friends would be anything but what it seemed.

It was the snowiest day of the year as they trekked the few blocks from their apartment to the restaurant, where Michael received a prearranged call from one of their supposed dinner guests.

"Looks like they're having car trouble and might not make it," Michael said, delivering the news to Sarah with a straight face. "Should we stay or go home?" he asked nonchalantly, hoping her answer would be the former.

"Let's stay," Sarah confirmed.

"Great." Michael exhaled, relieved that his plot was playing out flawlessly.

Once their plates had been cleared, Sarah and Michael headed out into the chilly March night again, but not before Michael furtively pulled out his BlackBerry and posted a status update on Facebook:

 Michael thinks Sarah should say yes.

Walking home, Michael set the next stage of his plan into motion. "Remember that first night, after dinner at the

General Greene, when I kissed you on the street? Maybe we should find that spot," Michael said, having previously spent hours scouting the exact location.

"Are you out of your mind? It's freezing!" Sarah exclaimed, standing in her long, bulky parka, her arms hugging her body.

"Indulge me," he replied, smiling and leading the way.

A few minutes later—having arrived at their destination—Michael faced Sarah, kissed her, and professed his abiding love and commitment to her, then handed her his BlackBerry with his Facebook status on the screen.

Perplexed, Sarah took the device, thinking: *Jesus Christ, he's got to show me that political piece he published today, right now, in the middle of the street on the snowiest night of the year! Couldn't it wait until we got home?*

But before she could protest, Sarah's eyes fell on Michael's post, and when she looked up again, Michael was down on one snow-sodden knee, proffering a vintage-inspired, platinum ring, with a significant emerald-cut diamond surrounded by two trapezoid rubies on either side.

"So, will you marry me?" He smirked at the irony.

"Yes!" Sarah shrieked, crying and jumping up and down.

At home, they called Sarah's parents—only to tell them about the engagement—still keeping the surprise nuptials mum. And Michael updated his Facebook status once more:

STATUS *Update*

 Michael is pleased to announce that Sarah said yes!

On Monday, March 9, 2009—six months to the day after their first date, and nineteen years after their initial meeting—Michael and Sarah tied the knot at New York's City Hall, with their parents as their witnesses.

But, after all, marriage is about compromise.

So, five months later, they did it all over again. On October 3, at The Woolverton Inn—across the Delaware River from the site of their former summer camp—Sarah walked down the aisle in a floor-length, champagne-hued silk and chiffon halter dress, adorned by a long, luxurious vintage necklace on a chain of faceted blue beads. It was the traditional ceremony and reception that Michael had wanted—with one hundred of their loved ones gathered around.

"We're so happy it's kind of ridiculous," says Sarah, who recently launched a fabulous floral design business—Blossom and Branch—in Brooklyn. "It took almost two decades, but we're finally together, which is exactly where we want to be."

FOUR

TALKING *On-Air*

*W*hen Sara Haines packed up her life and moved from her hometown of Newton, Iowa, to the Big Apple in the fall of 2000, she had one goal in mind: to become an actress.

A graduate of the esteemed Seven Sisters school, Smith College, Sara knew she wasn't cut out to bartend or waitress in order to make ends meet while she immersed herself in improvisation classes and auditions. So, she decided to use her liberal arts degree to land a day job as an archive assistant at a small production company, her first foot in the notoriously slammed-in-your-face door of the entertainment industry.

Sara feared she was casting too wide a net from the get-go, but rationalized that any job even remotely related to media would be, if nothing else, a valuable learning experience and an opportunity for her to feel out the trade.

Each day, she commuted two and a half hours by train from her apartment in Central New Jersey (Manhattan real estate was well beyond her financial reach) and, each day, she repeated the same mundane tasks at work: scanning records and creating online files that no one would ever read. It was so far from where she wanted to be, but there was nothing she could do about it, except look for alternate employment to fill the same temporary void.

One morning, on her usual train ride into the City, Sara spotted a gentleman two rows ahead of her with an NBC computer bag at his feet. During her initial quest for employment, she'd applied to the network's Page Program—a set of entry-level jobs for bright-eyed recent college graduates looking to break into television, whether for production, editing, public relations, or merely the bragging rights of pursuing a "sexy" career. *How awesome would it be to work in the same building where* Saturday

Night Live *is filmed? Or, even better, to rub elbows with the likes of Conan O'Brien or Tom Brokaw?* she'd thought.

But she hadn't heard back from NBC, and, as she observed the gentleman—considering the possibility of approaching him—her heart raced. *Could she ask him about the Page Program?* Her Midwestern roots even provoked the question: *What if I scare him because I'm approaching him in New York City?* Never did it occur to her that, as a young girl on a commuter train, the likelihood of frightening him was zero to none.

For three days, Sara shadowed her prey, gathering the nerve to introduce herself, until finally she knew it was then or never. Any day, she thought, he could switch his schedule and her prospect would be lost. As the train pulled into Penn Station and he stepped onto the platform, Sara rushed after him, tapping him gently on the shoulder.

"Excuse me. I'm, um, really sorry to bother you. My name is Sara. I just graduated from college. I'm here from Iowa. I don't want to scare you, but I'm trying to get into the NBC Page Program and I haven't had any luck getting through to anyone. I saw your computer bag and, well . . ."

"Let me give you my card," he replied, without hesitation. "You can send me your résumé, and I'll pass it along internally."

"Thank you so much!" Sara beamed, folding the card into her palm. She couldn't get to her current job fast enough to start the process of facilitating her departure.

FACEBOOK *Fairytales*

A week later, her résumé had fallen into the right hands, and, as frigid temperatures threatened to invade New York, there was a fire within Sara that couldn't be extinguished. Returning to her desk one afternoon at work, she noticed a missed call on her cell phone—it was a message from NBC about setting up an interview! But when Sara phoned back, her flame was temporarily squelched.

"They literally just announced a hiring freeze for pages. If you come in and meet with someone now, they're going to forget about you." The woman's voice was firm.

For the next five months, Sara called back nearly every week, occasionally getting waylaid by discouragement, and, by the time warm weather had insulated the City once more, she finally got the answer she'd been waiting for.

"We got the green light! You should come in."

After a series of exacting interviews, Sara received a letter in the mail stating she'd been accepted. And, in May 2001, overwhelmed with joy, she officially became an NBC page, working tirelessly for the next ten months, through September 11, a truly intense and historical time to be part of 30 Rock.

Until March 2002, when—on assignment at *Last Call with Carson Daly*—Sara received some intriguing news. One of her managers, who'd been continually impressed with her hard work and resolve, had submitted her name for a position as production coordinator at *The Today Show*. Sara, who'd been one of the only pages uninterested in the perpetual pursuit of a promotion, landed the job despite her feelings of relative ambivalence. It was one thing to spend a year learning the ropes of television; it was another to specialize herself even more, thus deviating further from her ultimate goal: to be in front of the camera.

But, with no acting gigs to speak of, Sara thought, *Okay, I'll try it. It's freelance for a year. We'll see what happens after that.*

One year passed as Sara took on any number of responsibilities for *The Today Show* guests—handling everything from cars, security, catering, hair, makeup, and wardrobe, to concerts on the plaza and VIP lists; there were more facets to her job, it seemed, than hours in the day to get them done. And, even though she had some time to audition on the side, her acting always played second fiddle to the main event—her day job.

Sara's boss, who'd been trying to secure her a staff position—the proverbial golden ticket—continued to encourage her not to leave, saying, "If you don't have another job, and you're just going to audition, it wouldn't hurt for you to stay another month," which quickly turned into, "Why don't you just stay until Christmas?"

Soon enough, Sara was offered a staff job, and by the fall of 2007, six years after her induction into the world of television, she finally took a step back and assessed her professional career—as best she could—from the outside looking in. Sure, she held an enviable position. And sure, she adored her day-to-day duties and the colleagues that surrounded and supported her. But could it be that she was in a rut—stuck on a career path she hadn't really wanted to walk down in the first place? More to the point, was there a light at the end of this tunnel—a way to parlay her experiences into something she'd be content with in the long term?

Realizing she craved forward momentum, Sara began pitching more and more ideas for segments in daily meetings, something she'd done often in the hopes of maximizing her time at the network. And, one day, short on staff, one of Sara's assigning producers said, "I like that idea. Can you produce it?"

"Absolutely!" Sara replied instantly, even though she'd never produced a segment in her life and had little idea how to do so. From that point on, Sara produced occasional segments and helped out on others, continually telling herself, *I might as well get the most out of this while I'm here.*

Not long after, *The Today Show* launched a website that required additional content, and everyone had more work piled on their plates. But instead of complaining about her extra tasks and longer hours, Sara saw an opportunity. She thought, *When the producers are stretched too thin, I can jump in and assist. Even better, I can put myself on camera*—which is precisely what she did.

Her first interview, with Five for Fighting front man John Ondrasik, was just the beginning, and even though her pieces were buried on the website's blog, her talent didn't go unnoticed. In 2008, *The Today Show* branded "Backstage Pass," with Sara leading the charge. It was still far from on-air, however, and Sara struggled to find a means of breaking through.

A few weeks later, with the knowledge that music sensation Chris Brown was set to appear on the show, Sara laid the groundwork for a plan, brainstorming with her fellow "Backstagers" about how to land her own interview with Chris.

The following morning, at 5 A.M., Sara and her skeleton crew—one coworker and an intern—awaited Chris Brown's appearance, under the watchful eyes of his bodyguard, Big Pat, when a novel idea popped into her head.

"This is our guy," Sara whispered to her team, motioning to Big Pat. "If we can't interview the talent, at least we'll have material."

What Sara couldn't have anticipated was that partway through her interview, Chris Brown would materialize, jumping up and down in front of the camera and subsequently answering questions post-concert.

Not only was she pleased with herself, but when she found out the website wouldn't be using the content, she came up with an alternate strategy—to go directly to NBC's in-house advertising department.

"I know you have a fan page on Facebook for *The Today Show*," she said. "Do you guys ever need extra content? I have some Chris Brown footage that I think you might like."

"Yes! We would love that!" Their response was exactly what Sara had hoped for. "We only use what we get from the show, but we don't have anything original."

"Great!" Sara felt an immediate sense of gratification.

Two weeks later, the ad agency's senior vice president called Sara and her team to his office and presented a graph representing the number of hits on *The Today Show*'s Facebook fan page.

"See, every time something big happens—like when Meredith Vieira joined the show—there's an equally big spike," he explained, motioning to an acme on the graph. "This jump here," he continued, pointing to the tallest summit, "is your Chris Brown video segment."

Sara's eyes widened. Her segment had more than tripled the highest peak they'd ever seen! She immediately marched straight into executive producer Jim Bell's office to inform him of her impressive feat.

"Wow! That's great!" he said, giving Sara the go-ahead to produce more and more content for their Facebook page.

Ultimately, Sara had to acknowledge one obvious pitfall: Not everyone was on Facebook. She needed to draw people to the social networking site in order for her segments to receive the viewership they so deserved.

She went back to Jim and said, "We've got these videos, and they're getting a lot of attention on Facebook, but our audience doesn't know they're there. Do you think I could tease them on the show?"

"Sure!" he agreed. "Then we can put your videos on *The Today Show* website."

Sara knew it was important to keep Facebook in the loop. Not only did they have a huge international web of connections, but also a demographic that would be lost on the main *Today Show* site. Additionally, they'd already gained momentum on the Facebook fan page and wanted as many eyeballs as possible on their content. So, she talked him into letting her keep Facebook on their hand-outs—with Backstage Pass and TodayShow.com appearing on the front, with the statement, "You can also find us on Facebook" on the back.

In August of 2008, Sara did her first on-air segment, which went well, prompting Jim to offer, "If you continue to bring me content, I'll continue to let you tease it on-air." And each week, that's exactly what she did.

Sara and her team had instigated a grassroots effort within the structure of a corporate conglomerate—with Jim bolstering them every step of the way.

Five months later, Sara got her first big break. It was the beginning of 2009, when Hoda Kotb and Kathie Lee Gifford, cohosts for the fourth hour of *Today*, mentioned to Sara, "We want you to appear on-air with us."

Sara could hardly believe her luck. Without delay, she kicked off intermittent appearances as their online "guru"—teaching people how to download photos off their cameras or demonstrating how to use a flash drive. Eventually, her sporadic gig transformed into bimonthly segments dubbed "Today's Tech."

What else can I do? Sara began asking herself, when it occurred to her and some of her colleagues that Kathie Lee and Hoda could use their very own Facebook page—as opposed to *The Today Show* fan page, which was inundated with three hours of news prior to them even going live.

With the help of Facebook executives, Sara worked assiduously to create and design every aspect of the page until February 5, when the big reveal would take place on the show's fourth hour.

In front of millions of viewers, Sara expertly enlightened Kathie Lee and Hoda on the specifics of Facebook, encouraging their audience at the same time: "If you guys out there are on Facebook, please search for Kathie Lee and Hoda and become a fan of our Facebook page."

Within minutes, Sara punched the refresh button on her laptop and their followers had jumped from 6 to 500. Everyone was astonished.

Once the cameras were off, the producer pulled Sara aside, asking, "Will you come on tomorrow? We want you to read some fan posts." By Thursday of that week, it was, "You do realize we're going to do this every day." And, one week later, "You do realize we're going to do this at the top and bottom of every show."

Slowly, Sara began to understand that acting might not be in the stars for her anymore, and she started pursuing full-time hosting jobs. Obviously *The Today Show* would never hire her as talent, she told herself. No one went from production coordinator to host without extensive experience.

A few months later, she'd gotten nowhere fast. Sara seriously started contemplating a Plan B. Perhaps she should abandon entertainment altogether and become a teacher. After all, she couldn't support herself on her current salary for the duration of her professional life.

Sharing her thoughts with a colleague, Sara sighed heavily, considering her prospects. Then her friend pointed out the obvious: "If you leave here without at least asking if they'd hire you to be on-air, you're going to regret it."

Even though Sara was certain she already knew the answer, later that afternoon she approached Jim tentatively. "Would you ever put me on the air?"

"I'm pretty sure I already have."

"No, I mean every day," she nudged.

"Sara, I've already done that. I don't understand your question," he laughed.

Then it occurred to her: He wasn't saying no. But what exactly was he saying yes to?

On May 21, 2009, Sara had her answer. The blonde-haired, blue-eyed, Newton, Iowa, transplant was officially promoted to full-time NBC talent. And, the following day, standing alongside her fellow *Today Show* cohosts, Sara was welcomed into the family fold—on-air—precisely where she'd always dreamed of being.

"I wouldn't be where I am today without the unconditional support of *Today*'s executive producer, Jim Bell," Sara insists, adding, "I'm also absolutely indebted to Facebook; without them, I wouldn't have had a daily excuse to appear on the show in the first place!"

FIVE

DESPERATELY SEEKING *Sister*

*I*t was 1961, in the small town of Dunkirk, New York, on the shores of Lake Erie, when Linda and Buddy Balzer welcomed their first child into the world—a baby girl named Deb. Two years later, their second daughter, Renee, was born.

Three years after that, they decided to split up. At the time, nobody really talked about divorce, especially in the predominantly Catholic area where the Balzers resided. It was one of those taboo subjects that parents of the '60s generation generally swept under the rug with the rest of their family crises. And once Deb's mother had been excommunicated from the church for this very reason, there was even further motive to maintain a low profile.

By 1972, Deb's father—whom she rarely communicated with—was already remarried with a third child—a daughter, Stacy, whom Deb knew nothing of. Shortly thereafter, Buddy's second marriage ended, and his contact with all three of his girls dwindled. Everyone went on with their lives, the Balzer girls being raised predominantly by their respective mothers—Deb and Renee together, Stacy on her own. None of them spoke of their father.

Life continued on like this until Deb was fourteen, when her curiosity got the best of her, and she showed up on Buddy's doorstep to confirm he hadn't passed away. After all, she hadn't heard from him in years—anything could have happened—and she had to see for herself that he was alive and well, even if he didn't want a close relationship with her.

It was then that Buddy informed Deb of his third daughter, Stacy. From this point on, she knew she had a second sister out there somewhere. But because of the era in which they were raised, and the fact that they were so young, Deb, Renee, and Stacy remained apart, leading separate lives into adulthood.

Twelve years later, on February 15, 1992, Deb received heartbreaking news. Her father had died at the age of fifty-two, and she had been named his next of kin. Now living in Minnesota, just under a thousand miles away from her New York roots, Deb flew home for the funeral, as did her sister Renee, from her family's home in Wilmington, North Carolina. They knew there was this sister, Stacy—eleven and nine years their junior, respectively—but they hadn't the faintest idea of how to reach her. *Did she even know her father had passed away?*

Deb decided to write Stacy's mother a letter:

My name is Deb Balzer, and I'm your daughter Stacy's older half-sister—born to Buddy and Linda Balzer in 1961. She also has a sister Renee, who's two years younger than me. Incidentally, Stacy and Renee share the same middle name—Lyn—as does Renee's only daughter, Alex Lyn.

Maybe Stacy will someday want to know that she has sisters. If so, please tell her that she's welcome to be in touch. We'd love to connect with her after all this time.

Deb did not receive a response. In her heart and mind, she realized that perhaps Stacy's mother had never told Stacy about her lineage, or that she had two sisters. Maybe she'd been raised by a stepfather and didn't even know who Buddy Balzer was. Not wanting to shake the apple tree, Deb abandoned hope and went on with her life—still with a small void that would likely remain empty.

Seventeen years passed. Then one day, in early 2009, Deb—a PR and marketing manager for the Animal Humane Society—was sitting in her office at work, deciding whether or not to take the plunge and join Facebook. She'd been hearing about it constantly in the news, and from her colleagues and friends. She had checked out some of the other social networking sites but found they weren't her style. Facebook, she noticed, seemed more closely targeted to her generation. So, she signed up, making sure that her privacy settings were airtight. She just wanted to get her feet wet, not dive in headfirst, and if she could search for other people without anyone being able to find her, that was good enough to start.

It was the year of Deb's thirtieth high school reunion— one of her incentives for joining Facebook in the first place—and as she searched the site for her former classmates, she came across the name of a girl she remembered fondly—Rosalie Gambino. Rosalie, Deb recalled, had been the first person who'd approached her when she'd been a new student at Fredonia High School, and they'd promptly become good friends.

Deb sent her first friend request to Rosalie, and progressed with her investigation. What was the point in being on Facebook, she reasoned, if she wasn't going to connect with people? She was apt to receive nothing more than some quick "catch-up" messages, and that was fine with Deb.

On the evening of January 22, the eldest sister of three received a note from her former friend Rosalie:

Deb,

I got this message from a girl named Stacy Balzer today. She said she's looking for you, but can't find you on Facebook. You can do what you want with it. Let me know if I can help. The message is pasted below.

Rosalie

Hello, Rosalie—

This is going to sound insane, but I did a Web search on Deb Balzer, and found that she'd posted a comment to the Fredonia High School site right after yours, which referenced Facebook. Then I went on Facebook and noticed that she's one of your friends, though I can't find her. Do you know if she deleted her profile?

I would really truly and greatly appreciate your help! You see, Deb is my half-sister. I haven't seen her since I was about one year old. I've been trying to find her and my other sister Renee for many years, with no luck.

I would never ask you to give out her information, but could you maybe let her know I'm on Facebook and would love some contact? I really hate imposing like this, but I thought, Hey! Facebook! Networking site! Maybe this avenue could work!

You really have no idea what it would mean to me . . .

Stacy Balzer

Deb read each word repeatedly—her heart sprinting—and thought, *I have to find this girl!* She immediately searched "Stacy Balzer" on Facebook and wrote to her:

Hello,

Are you the daughter of Sheila and Buddy Balzer? If so, I am your sister, Deb, and I would love to hear from you. If I have the wrong Stacy, my apologies.

Thank you,

Deb

Moments later, Deb had her answer:

Hello, Deb!

I am :) YAY for Facebook!

I swear, I cried yesterday afternoon when I found that nice Christmas card you sent me after Buddy passed away. Sorry, but I've never called him Dad, and actually never even knew what he looked like until about seven years ago when one of my aunts died and I was going through her photo albums. At that time I was just too shocked I guess, too hurt, too young to respond. And since then I've tried to find you through the Internet.

I don't know if you would like a relationship or not, but I would love to have my sisters in my life, finally. I feel like we missed out on so many things. Yes, mostly because of my mom and her not wanting me to have contact with Buddy, but I would really, really like to be a part, no matter how small, of your life!

Okay, here I go crying again! These 30-something hormones are for the birds, I swear!

Stacy

Still in shock, Deb called her sister Renee to fill her in. And, before long, Deb and Stacy were communicating, not only via Facebook, but also over the phone. At first, Deb was nervous that they'd have nothing to say. *Just because we're related by blood, doesn't mean we're going to like each other,* Deb reasoned. But her fear was laid to rest instantly when she and Stacy hit it off like best girlfriends. And, every Sunday for the ensuing months, the three sisters chatted frequently, updating each other on their lives to date.

In May, having had her fill of the long-distance relationship, Deb decided it was time for a belated reunion.

"You know, we can sit and talk all the time," she said, during their weekly call. "But wouldn't it be better to get together? Why don't you two come here for a short weekend over the summer?"

The response from her sisters was favorable, and Deb took her plan one step further.

"Why don't we make it a holiday weekend? Say, the Fourth of July? If all else fails, at least we can go see the fireworks together!"

Everyone was in agreement. Stacy would fly in from Montrose, Colorado, on the third, and Renee would arrive the next morning from North Carolina. They could barely wait the two months before seeing each other.

On July 3, at the Minneapolis-St. Paul International Airport, Deb waited at the gate, anxious to reunite with the sister she hadn't seen for nearly forty years. And when the door opened, Stacy ran toward Deb, embracing her, as the two laughed and cried simultaneously. That day and night, everywhere they went—from the shops to the Japanese restaurant—they shared their story with anyone who'd listen.

"We're sisters and we just re-met! No, really, we haven't seen each other in almost four decades. Can you believe it?"

Back at Deb's house that evening, she showed Stacy family photo albums she'd never known existed, and even presented her with her birth certificate—all of which had been given to Deb when their father had passed away. They didn't discuss what had happened to separate them all those years ago, but they both took solace in the fact that—despite Buddy's absence in their lives—their father had obviously loved them very much.

The following morning, Deb and Stacy headed back to the airport for a second reunion—at least for Stacy—with Renee. Deb, the mother hen of the bunch, was worried that her sisters might not hit it off, Stacy being more effusively affectionate, and Renee being traditionally more reserved. Not to mention the fact that Renee's non-tech-savvy existence had meant she'd communicated with Stacy less frequently.

But, as soon as Stacy and Renee met, Deb realized her concern had been unnecessary.

As they huddled close together, Renee laughed, saying, "I'm the tallest," standing at five-foot-three to Stacy's five feet and Deb's five-foot-two and three-quarters. The three sisters spent the rest of their short time together gossiping, sharing boisterous meals, celebrating with friends at a July 4th cookout, and—on Sunday—catching a matinee of Cirque du Soleil's *Kooza*.

As the weekend came to a close, Deb, Renee, and Stacy were reluctant to part ways. It had taken so long for them to reunite—the last thing they wanted to do was to splinter off again. "Let's do this next July Fourth, too," Renee declared. "It doesn't mean we can't see each other beforehand, but this will be our annual commitment. And you'll all come to North Carolina to visit me and my husband and our kids. Remember, Stacy's not only a sister; she's an aunt!"

These days, Deb—who has nearly 300 Facebook friends and has opened up her page so anyone can find her—is relishing her role as the oldest of three girls. "We all text each other at least five times a day, even Renee, who doesn't have e-mail!" she reveals. "Truly, the best part of all of this, though, was seeing my two younger sisters hit it off so easily."

And, when July 4th rolls around again, and again, and again . . . one thing's for sure—you'll find the Balzer sisters together, no matter where they are.

SIX

MISSING *Person*

*W*hen sixteen-year-old French student Tom Baraize was recruited to act as liaison officer for the Nepali Ski Team at the World Ski Championships in February 2009, he had no idea of the drama that would ensue.

Hailing from the quiet community of Lyon, in south-eastern France, roughly a ninety-minute drive from Val d'Isère—the legendary ski area in the French Alps where the championships would take place—Tom was excited and prepared for his many responsibilities to follow.

The Nepal Alpine skiing team, he was told, had been founded in 1997 by British businessman and former skier Richard Morley at the request of the Himalayan country's then ruler, King Birendra. Tom would report to Richard, the team's coach, and help him tend to the practical needs of the three skiers competing: their star, Shyam Dhakal; their number two, Subash Khatri; and their final and youngest recruit, sixteen-year-old Uttam Rayamajhi.

Tom, who was quadrilingual—speaking English, French, German, and Spanish—was assigned two significant tasks. His first and most important priority was to help the organization committee welcome the international teams; his second was to set up and manage the Nepali team's website.

Arriving in Val d'Isère, Tom was instantly swept up in the frenetic energy palpable at every turn. There were races, events, music, parties, food, and throngs of fans, skiers, and workers buzzing around the cool, sun-soaked slopes. It was a sixteen-year-old's dream job, and Tom could hardly believe his good fortune in landing it.

Tom hit it off immediately, not only with the team members, but also Coach Richard Morley. And as he ran around frantically dotting every "i" and crossing every "t" for the team—from transporting their gear to races and securing the proper documentation to getting them new ski equipment when theirs wasn't authorized—his friendships with the team members were cemented even further. Tom oversaw and chatted with them by day, drank with them in the evenings, and—ultimately—became part of their intimate family.

When the Ski Championships finally came to a close—after two weeks of working and playing hard—Tom departed from the team's base in Les Arcs to return home to Lyon, promising to stay in touch with his newfound friends. They discussed reuniting for a ski trip or even to work on a film about the team. Tom felt gratified and lucky to have experienced this once-in-a-lifetime opportunity.

Nearly two months passed, and in April—back at home—Tom found a note from Richard in his Facebook in-box. *Perhaps he's writing to get together or to plan our ski trip*, Tom speculated, energized at the thought. He opened the message at once:

> *Tom,*
> *I have some disturbing news. Uttam Rayamajhi has vanished from the team's base at Les Arcs. No one knows where he's gone. Please let me know if you've heard anything.*
> *Regards,*
> *Richard*

Alarmed by word of his friend's disappearance, Tom hastily logged on to Facebook to connect with Richard.

They'd communicated via the social networking site often, and Tom knew that Richard would likely be on Facebook more often than on his regular e-mail, since it was the fastest and most efficient way of reaching as many people as possible at one time. Tom wrote:

Richard,

Please send me your number so we can chat via phone. I want to help in any way I can.

Sincerely,

Tom

Minutes later, Tom and Richard were speaking directly, and Richard was explaining the circumstances surrounding Uttam's departure from the team's base camp. Uttam, Richard said, had been distraught because of the disintegration of Nepal's ski team in the wake of a funding debacle. Essentially, a corrupt Nepali leader had rescinded his promise of financial support for the team, and when Richard had filed a complaint with the International Olympic Committee, not only had he been dismissed as coach, but the skiers' scholarships had been revoked—rendering Uttam inconsolable and the team's chances of competing in the 2010 Vancouver Olympics hopeless.

Confused and concerned, Tom had an idea. "I might have a way to find Uttam," he told Richard.

MISSING *Person*

Having been a member of Facebook for a year and a half, Tom was familiar with the viral effect of the site, and decided to start a group whose main purpose would be to help track down his forlorn friend. He titled it "Help Uttam and All Victims of Corruption in Sport," and included photos of Uttam, along with a full description of his story—in both French and English—on the opening page.

Aside from finding Uttam, Tom's secondary goal was to denounce the Nepali government's crooked behavior, and to fight to break the cycle of fraudulence in the sports arena. It was a lofty objective, perhaps, but this didn't stand in the sixteen-year-old's way.

Using the Facebook group as his platform, Tom swiftly spread information about Uttam's disappearance to all of his contacts, inviting them to join the group and asking them to invite their own friends to follow suit. He even included Uttam in his plea.

One week later, the group was 500 members strong. And when Tom sat down at his computer after school one afternoon, he noticed that Uttam had become a member of the very group designed to find him. There was no note or any indication of his whereabouts, but Tom and Richard—who he called immediately upon finding Uttam's response—were beyond relieved to learn that the young skier was alive and well. After all, he was only sixteen and had been missing for weeks—with no money, clothes, or telephone at his disposal.

But where was he? And why had he only accepted the Facebook request and not contacted someone—especially having seen the desperate online campaign to locate him?

They'd have their answers soon enough.

Once Richard had alerted the police, confirming that Uttam was in fact alive, and mass media had gotten wind of the news, Uttam—astonished by the spectacle of so much attention—contacted Richard, who took the first train to Paris to hear the young boy's side of the story.

Uttam had been wandering the streets of the City of Lights, near the Bastille, having hitchhiked there from Les Arcs with just five euros in his pocket. He'd been stopped by police a number of times, he said, but had produced a valid visa and been released. Nearly three weeks had gone by, and he'd been surviving on mostly bread, when a man—a stranger—had called out to him.

"Hey, kid! I saw you on Facebook," he'd declared, flagging Uttam down. "There's a group with photos of you and your story. They're looking everywhere for you."

Subsequently, the man had invited Uttam to come back to his house so he could see for himself. That was when Uttam had accepted Tom's invitation to the group.

"Why did you not call someone, or at least let us know you were okay?" Richard questioned.

"I had to take a step back and think about my life," Uttam revealed. "When they took away our funding, I realized that I'd wasted two years of my life pursuing a skiing career. I'd dropped out of school to train, and I just needed some time alone to let it all sink in. I felt discouraged and angry."

"I understand. We were all very frustrated, but you still should have come to me," Richard said, resting his hand on Uttam's shoulder. "That's what I'm here for."

"I know. And I'm sorry." Uttam smiled humbly.

"Will you come back with me?"

"Not just yet, but I will return to camp soon."

And that he did. A few days later, Uttam rejoined Richard and his fellow teammates in Les Arcs. He also wrote a long-overdue Facebook message to a very special friend:

Tom,

I cannot thank you enough for your help and attention in looking for me. You never abandoned hope, and, if not for the Facebook group, I may have been a lost soul forever.

Thank you.

Your friend always,

Uttam

While the future of the Nepali ski team remains ambiguous, Uttam is back in his home country, reenrolled in school and eagerly awaiting an opportunity to return to the slopes.

As for the story's hero, Tom Baraize, he says, "I'm quite proud of what I did, and I look forward to seeing my friends on the ski team again very soon. Maybe we can meet up for a drink when they come back to France."

How would Tom describe his experience at the World Championships in retrospect?

"Five words: Best time of my life."

SEVEN

PRESIDENTIAL *Coup*

*B*orn in the acutely conservative city of Hickory, North Carolina, Chris Hughes was a devoutly religious Southern boy, the only child of a paper salesman and a public-school teacher.

But his interests belied his roots, and when the time came for him to attend high school, Chris set his sights on the East Coast, specifically the distinguished prep school, Phillips Academy in Andover, Massachusetts—to which he received a munificent financial aid package that he couldn't pass up.

Four years later, Chris obtained a scholarship to Harvard, where—as luck would have it—whiz-kid-in-the-making Mark Zuckerberg and Dustin Moskovitz became his sophomore roommates.

By February 2004, Chris, Dustin, fellow classmate Eduardo Saverin, and Mark—who'd spent his winter vacation creating a basic website where people could share a little information about themselves, connect with friends at other colleges and universities, and do so in a trusted, local environment—had conceived the first incarnation of Facebook.

There was no wall. There were no photos. There wasn't even a means of exchanging messages. Yet, the four Ivy Leaguers knew they were on to something. Mark handled the coding, with help from Dustin. Eduardo managed business development and sales. And, Chris, who possessed little technical knowledge, worked on the functionality and building of the site. Together, through the spring, they worked tirelessly to advance the breadth of Facebook's purpose. And when the press started calling, having gotten wind of the social networking site's growing popularity, it was Chris who fielded the calls, acting as the start-up's spokesman.

PRESIDENTIAL *Coup*

Unlike Mark and Dustin, however, once it became clear that Facebook could no longer be run by four college students with full class schedules, Chris decided to make academics his priority. While two of his partners dropped out of school and headed to Palo Alto to cultivate the business, Chris remained at Harvard, determined to earn the diploma he'd worked so hard for.

But it was hardly the end of his Facebook involvement. Leading up to graduation, Chris commuted back and forth from Cambridge to California during the year and spent summers there, preparing to become a permanent staffer once his cap and gown had been achieved.

By 2006, around the time of the midterm elections, Chris was in full Facebook swing. They'd unveiled their service to the world and, in addition to his regular duties, Chris began managing the company's political product—a small box on users' profiles declaring their support for specific candidates, and allowing them to self-organize around a cause they believed in. This new responsibility—which landed him in Washington, D.C., from time to time, and initiated extensive interaction with those on Capitol Hill devoted to all things online—also facilitated his introduction to Jim Brayton, Barack Obama's Internet director.

And when it came time for the Illinois senator to make his formal bid for president of the United States, Jim offered Chris a once-in-a-lifetime opportunity: to join the campaign as director of online organizing. Of course, it meant he'd have to take a leave from his executive post at Facebook, but the decision was a no-brainer for the twenty-four-year-old. Chris realized it was a truly historical time in government, and—above all—possessed a profound respect for Barack Obama not only as a candidate, but for Barack Obama as an individual.

In February 2007, Chris left Facebook and its 15 million users to move to chilly Chicago, where he'd commence a unique experience that would alter the course of American politics indelibly. He believed in Barack Obama and his message of change, perhaps more than he believed in his own capabilities of tackling such a daunting task.

Arriving on the scene two weeks after the February 10th launch of Obama's own social network, MyBarackObama .com—the first of any presidential candidate—Chris hit the ground running with the support of a skeleton crew of three. The website—which invited supporters to build a profile, blog their campaign experiences, plan and attend events, enlist other supporters, and help raise funds for the campaign—was a heavy load to bear, and for the first few months, it was all hands on deck as they scrambled to maintain up-to-date status.

Chris and his team toiled day in and day out to generate enthusiasm across the country and to convert that energy—using every online tool they could get their hands on—into election day votes. The basic premise was to decentralize access to organizing tools, thereby making it possible for anyone, anywhere, to work on behalf of the campaign in their local community through the various platforms. Whether it meant knocking on doors or making phone calls, the idea was to beat campaign infrastructure to the punch, so that people didn't have to wait to be guided. It was "power to the people" in its truest form.

Over the course of the next eighteen months, Chris and his colleagues plugged away, continually upgrading the technology in an effort to really help people feel they were a part of the larger picture. And, before long, presidential hopeful Barack Obama was starting to notice the results, stopping in when time permitted to encourage Chris and to communicate directly with widespread grassroots organizers through conference calls, videos, and his ever-resourceful staff.

Outside of MyBarackObama.com, Chris also managed a text-messaging program for those who favored mobile devices to computers, and oversaw presences on various previously established social networking sites, such as MySpace, BlackPlanet, and, naturally, Facebook—the central focus being to provide access to organizing tools so that individuals could work for the campaign remotely, and, consequently, garner more votes for Obama.

Perhaps due to Chris's familiarity and long-standing connection with the website, Facebook was a key component in this effort. The platform, whose basic premise is to connect individuals across the globe, simply made sense in its new context. But, while it fostered the necessary communication, that wasn't enough. Chris knew he needed to give

Facebook members something to talk about, and, moreover, to make it as simple as possible for them to do so.

Fortunately, he had a buzz-worthy candidate to promote, a fact that made his job that much easier. With no shortage of excitement surrounding Barack Obama's every move, Chris set out to take advantage of the hype—to mobilize Americans to get out and vote, particularly young people who might not have voted before, and to make sure that their peers and their parents did the same thing. He knew it was all about connecting the dots between online action and votes on election day.

But he also knew how easy it was for people to get distracted by all of the cool things to do online. So he channeled his attention into a few key Facebook strategies: the development of a Barack Obama fan page; the oversight of thousands of local groups; and the creation of a computer application. All three facets, he hoped, would work in tandem toward the overriding goal—victory for their candidate.

Facebook quickly became a second hub of the campaign, where anyone who was interested in Barack Obama could become a supporter. Chris and his team could then communicate directly with those people, systematically informing them of the goings-on in the campaign. If there was an interesting video, they'd send it out, asking users to post it to their own profiles. If they needed everyone to donate $10, or make ten phone calls, or host a party in their dorm room or home, they could use the page to promote it. Whatever was problematically most important, at any given moment, said predicament could be solved using Facebook.

Another vital component was the website's well-known news-feed feature. Chris and his troops worked to get as many people as possible at one time to RSVP to their events or to join one of their support groups, rationalizing that the news feed was centered on trending stories. Therefore, if several of an individual's friends were concentrating on the same thing—namely, Barack Obama—that individual would more likely be exposed to the story in their own feed, thus making it that much easier for people who weren't as familiar with Barack Obama to acquire information. And if, in a best-case scenario, all of these individuals joined one of the groups, Chris could message them to his heart's content about everything that the campaign was doing on a local level.

As if that weren't enough, Chris and his squad established an application on Facebook that was capable of presenting all manner of content produced by the campaign—videos, blogs, photos, commentaries, e-mails—basically anything and everything they could use to their advantage. People could acknowledge what they liked most, thereby elevating that content to the top of the page. Additionally, this impelled friends to alert other friends in battleground states.

One might log on to the platform application, view a video, and give it the famous Facebook "thumbs-up."

They would then be prompted with a strategically crafted question: "Would you like to send this video to your friend who lives in Iowa and is not yet a supporter?" The domino effect was priceless.

By the end of the campaign—in part, because of Chris's brilliant tactics—the social networking site he had cofounded had fashioned Facebook Connect, which made it possible for people to identify and target their friends in swing states, and, most important, to register to vote on the spot. If you logged on to MyBarackObama.com, you could even link it to your Facebook account. As a result, everything you did on the site—if you donated money, called constituents, or joined a group—would then show up on Facebook.

Chris was on top of the world as the fruits of his labor were realized on the international landscape: 2 million profiles had been created on the site; 200,000 offline events had been organized; 35,000 groups had been formed; 400,000 posts had been blogged; and $30 million had been generated on 70,000 personal pages. On Facebook alone, Barack Obama had roughly 5 million supporters. And the most staggering statistic of all: the $500 million raised through 3 million unique donors, by Obama's New Media group—for which Chris had helmed the organizing arm.

But the real coup was still to come.

On November 4, 2008, Barack Obama won the presidency, with 52.9 percent of the popular vote and 365 electoral votes, to become the first African American elected to the office. As he delivered his victory speech before hundreds of thousands of supporters in Chicago's Grant Park, Chris Hughes swelled with satisfaction and pride.

And on January 20, 2009, when the former junior senator from Illinois was inaugurated as the 44th president of the United States, Chris Hughes—the Southern boy with the conservative roots—officially became a Democratic hero.

After the campaign was over and the hoopla had died down, Chris packed his bags and headed to New York City, where he worked remotely for a Boston-based venture capital firm. He also reunited with Facebook—the company that had paved his political path—staying up-to-date with their progress, but not involving himself in day-to-day decision making.

"I think the introduction of social networking to Barack Obama's campaign was an unequivocal piece of the puzzle," says Chris, who was featured on the cover of the April 2009 issue of *Fast Company* magazine under the headline, THE KID WHO MADE OBAMA PRESIDENT, a title he hardly feels comfortable with.

"I sort of recoil at that label because it's simply not accurate. It was the whole team—the people that I was lucky enough to have worked with—that had a real impact on the election."

What's next for our modest protagonist?

"I'm looking to start something new or to join a start-up. I really love building things from the ground up, and there are a lot of interesting things happening in New York right now."

But what about Washington? Would Chris consider resuming his post for our president's incumbent race?

"I think I've spent my time in politics. I had a lot of fun doing it, and while it's highly unlikely I'd go back, I wouldn't trade my experience for the world."

EIGHT

DRINING *Force*

*I*t was November of 2005, just before Thanksgiving, when Brian Hickey lost his mother to a brain tumor. He'd married his bride, Angela, only four months prior, and their first holiday together as husband and wife was overcast with a dark shadow of grief.

Three years later, around the same time of year, Brian's sadness was still palpable. Eager to find a bright spot during an otherwise dreary stretch, he was looking forward to meeting up with a group of old high school friends in the town where he'd grown up, for Thanksgiving and subsequently Black Friday.

Angela, who was working at the University of Pennsylvania supervising clinical research on breast cancer trials, was also attending school there full-time for her nursing degree.

"Is it okay if I stay home and study for finals?" she asked Brian at the last minute. He didn't mind. It would be a night out with the boys.

So, at 3:15 that Friday afternoon, Brian took the train into downtown Philadelphia and then hopped on the high-speed line to New Jersey, where he was hooking up with his buddies.

As a career journalist who'd spent years covering city crime in both New Jersey and Philadelphia, Brian knew how to get around. And at 4:45 P.M., he arrived at his destination, ready to kick off the night with Happy Hour.

At home hitting the books, Angela received a text from Brian around six o'clock. He said he was having a blast with his friends and wished she could be there. Angela sighed. She had plenty of work ahead of her and didn't expect Brian to be home until at least midnight, maybe even as late as two in the morning. Angela continued on with her Friday night, ultimately falling asleep amid her books.

She was sound asleep until 2:30 A.M., when she awakened to find that Brian hadn't come home yet. She called his cell. No answer. *Perhaps he's in a loud bar*, she thought. Angela left a message and fell back asleep.

Half an hour later, she woke up again, called Brian a second time, and left another voice message—this time more urgent. And every half-hour thereafter she repeated the process. *I'm sure he's gone to Atlantic City*, she told herself, when the fear crept up inside her.

But, at 5:30 in the morning, as the sun began to pierce through the dark night sky and Brian was still nowhere to be found, Angela had another thought. She knew Brian frequently checked his Facebook page from his Black-Berry, and even though she hadn't been a member for long, and it certainly wasn't a typical means of communication between them, she decided to log on and send him a note. She wrote: *I've been trying to reach you for hours and have left multiple messages. If you don't call me back, I'm going to have to call the hospital.*

She received no response. Angela even called their bank to see if he'd visited an ATM, in hopes they could shed even a little bit of light on Brian's whereabouts. There had only been one withdrawal, from 5 P.M. the previous day, and the sum hadn't been anything out of the ordinary.

At 7 A.M., with nowhere else to turn, Angela called Brian's father.

"Dan, I don't know what to do," she said. "I can't find Brian. He never came home last night. He doesn't answer his phone, and he hasn't returned any of my messages."

Concerned by the alarm in his daughter-in-law's voice, and desperate to track down his son, Dan helped Angela make calls to all of Brian's friends, namely the people they knew he'd been with the night before. But one dead end followed another. Some of his friends had decided not to meet up. One had had to work late. And another had been texting with Brian throughout the night when all of a sudden, Brian had stopped responding. No one knew where Brian was, but everyone joined the mission to help Angela and Dan find him.

Finally, with no leads to speak of, Angela logged on to AT&T's website to pull up their phone bill. Brian hadn't made a call since 10:07 P.M. the previous night, and he hadn't texted since around the same time. All she could find were a slew of incoming text messages and phone calls. She recognized a New York number that belonged to Brian's high school friend, Heather, and dialed it. Heather told Angela that she and some other friends had been with Brian until close to ten, at which time they'd split up and scattered to different parties.

"I'll make a few calls and get back to you," Heather said.

And by 10:30 A.M., Angela's phone rang, flashing Heather's number.

"Angie, don't freak out. Stay calm," she said. "One of Brian's friends just found out he's in the hospital. I don't know anything more than that, but I need your phone number because they're going to call you."

Within ten of the longest minutes of her life, Angela received a call from a trauma ICU nurse at Cooper University Hospital in Camden, New Jersey.

"Your husband is unconscious. We had to intubate him, and a ventilator is helping him breathe," she said. "We think he's either been beaten up or hit by a car. Please come here as quickly as possible."

Hysterical, Angela sped to the hospital—the same hospital where Brian's mother had passed away almost three years ago to the day.

Once there, talking to medics and police officers over the next twelve hours, Angela pieced together the puzzle—Brian had been on foot, walking along a one-lane, one-way residential street that ran the five blocks from the train station to the tavern where he'd been hanging out with friends. Because there were no sidewalks, Brian had been walking next to the parked cars, against traffic, and a car or truck must have hit him head-on.

Fortunately, the accident had taken place close to a streetlight and directly in front of one of the only homes that faced that side of the street. A twenty-one-year-old male college student who had been home that night watching movies had heard the collision, even though the driver had fled the scene. He'd called 911 and had, in all likelihood, given Brian his only chance at survival.

Angela entered the trauma ICU, and when she found Brian's bed, tears flooded her eyes. There were tubes down his throat and a catheter protruded from the right side of his head. The doctors had paralyzed him with drugs and administered medications to remove the fluid from his brain.

Brian's father arrived shortly thereafter. Angela could see the intense emotion on his face. Not only had he lost his wife a few years prior—in the very same hospital—but Brian was his only child. Angela hugged him tightly and reassured him, saying, "He's not going anywhere; that's too much pain for anyone to endure."

The doctors informed Angela and Dan that Brian had a left frontal lobe injury that had caused a subdural hematoma, subarachnoid hematoma, and multiple contusions. He had also fractured his T7 and T9 vertebrae. If the drugs he was being given didn't work, they said, Brian would need decompression surgery, where they'd cut the scalp and then cut pieces of his skull out to relieve the pressure from the fluid gathering around the brain. They were trying to prevent his brain stem from herniating, because once that happened, the patient was declared brain-dead.

"Your husband is young and doesn't have any health problems," the doctor said. "But the surgery is still a last resort."

Overwhelmed and fatigued, Angela made a brief trip home to feed and walk their dog, Charlie. She realized she needed to alert her friends and family to what had happened, but she didn't have the energy or emotional stability to make multiple phone calls. So she turned to Facebook once again, this time signing on to Brian's page, since—at 450 friends—his network of connections far exceeded hers. Angela posted her first of many status updates to come:

Brian needs your prayers. He was the victim of a hit-and-run last night at 10:15 P.M. in New Jersey. He's in the ICU with a subdural hematoma and cerebral contusions. Please pray for him.

Two hours later, as she was preparing to drive back for the second visiting hour of the day, Angela received a call from the doctor: "We need to do the surgery right away! The pressure in Brian's brain is spiking."

Angela rushed to the hospital again, but Brian had already been wheeled into the operating room. All she could do was wait and send another Facebook update. Her cell phone had been ringing off the hook and her voice mail was maxed out with messages. And even though she was on the phone constantly, answering her many calls, there was no possible way for her, physically or emotionally, to update everybody. Brian's friend list had nearly doubled almost instantly—jumping from 450 to 850—so Facebook swiftly became the easiest and most efficient way of communicating with everyone. The social networking site that Angela had barely used prior to Brian's accident ended up being her news-disseminating savior.

Brian's surgery was finished by 11:30 that night, and he was taken back to ICU where Angela was able to say a quick good-night to her husband.

Five days after the accident, the doctor told Angela that Brian likely wouldn't wake up for at least a month, if ever, and if he did wake up, they felt that due to the nature of his injuries, he probably wouldn't be able to move the right side of his body.

For the next several days, Angela would call the nurses' station at 6 A.M. every morning to check on Brian's progress, and after each conversation she would post the updates on Facebook—where he was on the coma scale, what his CAT scan results were, how stable he was, and what the physicians were doing to manage his recurring fevers.

By Saturday, only eight days after his accident, Brian opened his eyes for the first time, and Angela released her first true sigh of relief in over a week.

One month later, the day before he was to be moved to a rehab center across the Delaware River in Philadelphia, Brian had regained most of the movement on his left side. On his right side, he could only move his leg a couple of inches, and he still couldn't move his right arm at all. Nonetheless, Brian was silently determined to recuperate completely once his brain started working again. Soon, he was able to speak again for the first time, replying "journalist" when the doctor asked what he did for a living.

On December 18, Brian was finally discharged to rehab, with a long road to recovery ahead of him.

The next four weeks weren't easy—for Brian or Angela. Brian remained emotionally flat and, due to his brain injury, was, on occasion, belligerent when spoken to. Unlike Angela, he didn't shed a single tear; that part of his brain just wasn't working yet.

By Christmas Eve, Brian was able to walk a few dozen steps for the first time, and on Christmas Day, he moved his right arm, which was an exceptionally positive indication. He even signed a Christmas card with his left hand, despite being insistent that relearning to use his right—his writing hand—was the only option moving forward.

In the meantime, Angela returned Brian's BlackBerry to him in his hospital bed, in hopes of helping him learn to communicate again, even if he couldn't really write or speak yet. Almost immediately, he posted a status update to Facebook:

 Brian gets off on certain trouble.

It wasn't coherent, but he'd been able to construct a full sentence, which was significant.

Brian enthusiastically and reflexively assumed Angela's job as Facebook reporter to all of his 900 Facebook friends, which she gladly relinquished, pleased to see how happy this role made him and what a help it was throughout his recovery.

It wasn't until January 4, 2009, that Brian showed emotion for the first time. Angela walked into his room to find him crying hysterically. The magnitude of what had happened had finally hit him, and his tears were shed in happiness, not despair. *I'm alive*, he realized, *and I'm going to get better.*

Nearly two weeks later, on January 16, Brian was sent home from the rehabilitation center with a brace that covered him from his waist to his shoulders, and a helmet that he had to wear anytime he left his bed, until his final surgery on April 21, when the bones from his skull were to be put back in.

On February 2, Brian Hickey took to Facebook once more, but this time he wasn't updating his medical condition. The Philadelphia newspaper columnist and crime reporter was starting a Facebook page titled, "Help Me Find the Person Who Almost Killed Me." The introduction read: *On November 28th, I was nearly killed by a hit-and-run driver while walking to catch the train home. More than two months later, there's scant information coming from the public, and the person has yet to 'fess up. It's time for that to change.*

Since that time, Brian—who's nearly completely recovered following his surgery in April—has had a number of leads thanks to Facebook.

"I hope that what this guy or gal did haunts them until the day they die," Brian avows. "And I mean that, because I may forgive the driver for nearly killing me, but I'll never forgive them for what my wife had to go through."

NINE

ARE YOU MY *Father?*

*T*wenty-three years ago, in Edmonton—the capital of the Canadian province of Alberta—Jordan Luft was born to unwed teenagers Monica Kintop and Heath Reichle, neither of whom was prepared to be a parent.

Two weeks later, Monica and Heath turned their son over to a government agency, and Jordan was placed with an adoptive family—Doug and Connie Luft. No names were disclosed. No strings were attached.

Monica and Heath (who'd also been adopted as a child) knew they'd made the right decision for their baby boy. After all, they were still in high school and had no means of financial support. Their son would be better off with an older couple who could give him the love and attention he deserved, they reasoned, and—from that day on—they knew nothing of their son's whereabouts or the family who'd taken him in.

Meanwhile, two and a half hours south, in Didsbury— a small town in central Alberta, at the foothills of the Rocky Mountains—Jordan was growing up on Triple L Farms with his adoptive parents and extended family of twenty-seven first cousins. His life revolved around the eighty-year-old family farm, where they produced grain, wheat, hay, alfalfa, barley, and dairy products. Life was simple.

Jordan had always known he'd been adopted, though he hadn't given it much thought over the years. Sure, there'd been times he'd wondered about his background, mostly when it came to medical history, but, all in all, he was happy, cared for, and cherished by his adoptive parents. There was no reason to look any further.

Until one afternoon—when Jordan was eighteen—and his adoptive father, Doug, sat him down.

"I want you to know that you're old enough now to send your name to the Alberta Adoption Registry," he said, watching his son process the information. "All you have to do is sign a document saying that you'd like to find your birth parents, and if they've done the same thing, you'll be able to find out who they are. It's up to you. We're behind you no matter what you decide."

This was the first Jordan had heard of any such opportunity, and he wasn't sure how he felt about it. *Did he really need to know who his birth parents were? What if they wanted to meet him? What if he didn't like them? Or, worse, what if they didn't like him?* For days, questions deluged his mind, and, ultimately, he determined he just wasn't ready.

Two years passed and nothing more was said about it. Until one day, provoked by sheer curiosity, Jordan finally sent a letter to the adoption registry, requesting information on his genealogy.

A few months after that, a large envelope arrived in the mail. It contained Jordan's birth parents' names—Monica Kintop and Heath Reichle. It also listed another interesting fact: Jordan had been born Ryan Heath Kintop. Since his birth parents hadn't been married by law he'd been given Kintop—his birth mother's maiden name—as his surname.

Immediately, Jordan searched for Monica Kintop online, finding a few matches, but none that seemed to fit either the correct time or place. Stymied, he decided to look for his birth father instead. With two clicks of the mouse, he stared at the computer screen in front of him. There it was—as plain as day—his father's name, telephone number, and address. Heath Reichle was alive and well, still living in Edmonton, only a few hours from Jordan's family farm.

Jordan dialed the number, his hands shaking. He had no idea what he was going to say, or even *if* he'd be able to say anything. To his relief, the answering machine picked up.

"Um, hi," Jordan's nervous voice cracked. "I'm not trying to sell you anything. My name is Jordan Luft, and I have something I'd like to talk to you about. Here's my number. Please call me back."

Jordan hung up the phone, his heart beating rhythmically against his chest, and sat quietly for what felt like hours, waiting for a ring to pierce the silence.

It wasn't until the next day, however, that Heath returned the call. Jordan, seeing the number flash on his phone, felt far too anxious to pick up. But Heath left a message, one that indicated that he knew who Jordan was and the reason for his call. He didn't say as much, but the suggestion in his voice was tangible.

Jordan contemplated trying to contact Heath again, reconnecting to the roots from whence he'd come. Something stopped him, though, and for the next year, he buried the notion deep down inside, unsure as to whether he'd ever allow it to resurface.

And he may never have, if not for Facebook.

Having been a member of the social networking site for over a year, Jordan habitually logged on to update his status and read his friends' posts. One day, on a whim, he decided to search out a new friend: Heath Reichle. He couldn't believe it hadn't occurred to him before, but—pressing enter—he held his breath, anxious to see if there were any matches.

There were. One profile appeared. It was an older man and his resemblance to Jordan was uncanny. Noting that Heath was in Facebook's Edmonton network, Jordan joined and—for the first time in his life—was able to see photos of what he believed to be his birth father and extended family. In one particular photo caption, he noticed that Heath's middle name was Arnold. The packet of information Jordan had received from the adoption registry had listed his paternal grandfather's first name as Arnold. The writing was on the wall, but the question still remained: Was Jordan going to do anything about it?

At 4:23 in the morning, on June 6, 2008, he made up his mind. He'd come this far, and there was no turning back. Before he could change his mind again, Jordan sent a Facebook message to Heath Reichle:

Heath,

Would you mind if I ask if your middle name is Arnold?

Jordan

For the rest of the day, Jordan checked Facebook reflexively, but heard nothing back. He couldn't believe how excited he was at the prospect of connecting with his birth father, and—impulsively—he posted a status update to his page:

Jordan Luft is speechless. I think I found my birth father on Facebook.

Twenty-four hours later, Jordan had a message from Heath in his in-box:

Jordan,

Yes, Arnold is my middle name!

I was reading your profile, where you said you think you've found your birth father. Does that happen to have anything to do with this? If it does . . . AWESOME!

Would you like to know your birth mother's name? I hope this is why you contacted me.:)

Heath

And the conversation continued:
June 7, 11:58 A.M.

Heath,

Indeed. I called you about a year ago. You called back, and I let it ring through because I was pretty nervous. I had no idea how to act. Then, a few nights ago, I thought, Why not try Facebook? And sure enough, your name was the only one that came up. We look nearly identical. Yeah, it's pretty AWESOME. One big thing I want to ask . . . I see you're married with a family now. Is it going to be an issue if we talk?

Jordan

June 7, 2:14 P.M.

Jordan,

No issue whatsoever! I thought that was you on the phone last year. I was also nervous and wanted to contact you again, but figured it would be better to let you reach out to me in your own time.

Monica, your birth mother, and I aren't together anymore. We broke up about two years after you were born. It was probably for the best but we did remain friends for quite some time. I lost touch with her about 10 years ago, but I know she would LOVE to chat with you. We really didn't want to give you up for adoption, but we knew it was for the best since we were so young. We had prayed that you would be placed in a loving home and always wondered how you were.

My wife Tracey has been pushing me to try to contact you, but—like I said—I figured when YOU were ready you could contact me. ;) As you can see in our photos, you have three half-brothers (19, 18, and 17), one half-sister (6), and two step-siblings, a girl (14) and a boy (9).

I am just SOOOOO happy that you finally contacted me. It's been killing me inside. I have so much to tell you and so much to ask you. My heart is just POUNDING.

Whenever you are ready to call me or meet me, just ask. In the meantime, I'll try to get in touch with Manfred (Monica's brother), but will let you contact her when you are ready.

Take care, and hope to chat with you again soon.

Heath ARNOLD Reichle

June 7, 3:13 P.M.

Heath,

It's been over 22 years, and if you're up for it, I'll drive up there. Let's make this happen!

To answer quickly, I was raised in a HUGE loving family. Thank you for making such a responsible choice.

Well, now my heart is pounding hard too.

Ciao,

Jordan

With several days' worth of messages exchanged, the following Saturday, Jordan finally gathered the nerve to call Heath, and couldn't have been more pleased with the outcome. Not only did their voices sound identical, but they also shared a remarkably similar sense of humor. It was breathtaking for both of them.

"For the past twenty-two years, every April eighth, I've celebrated your birthday," Heath told Jordan. "All of your brothers and sisters have been thrilled at the prospect of meeting you one day."

And then he surprised Jordan with the best news of all.

"I found Monica. She's remarried, living not far from here. She and her husband have two young daughters. You're going to have an even bigger family!"

Overjoyed, and with the full support of his adoptive parents, Jordan made up his mind to drive to Edmonton the next weekend to finally—after more than two decades—meet the man and woman who'd reluctantly given him up all those years ago.

On Father's Day weekend, 2008, Jordan reunited with both of his birth parents in quick succession—Heath on Saturday, and Monica on Sunday. Things went so well, in fact, that one week later Jordan moved from Didsbury to Edmonton to reap the fruits of his family tree.

These days, he can be found spending copious amounts of time with both his adoptive and his birth parents, while he earns his college degree at the Northern Alberta Institute of Technology.

"It's funny; the other day, Heath said to me, 'I can't believe, after all this time, we were reunited—just like that—through something as simple as Facebook!'" Jordan laughs. "I can tell you one thing for sure: We all feel very, very grateful."

TEN

HELLO,
Mr. Prime Minister

$\mathcal{I}$t was election time in Denmark. Claus Drachmann—a schoolteacher in the picturesque township of Mariager—sat at his desk contemplating the political climate, as his fellow Danes flocked to parks and beaches, determined to take advantage of the fleeting warm weather.

As Claus idly skimmed his Facebook page, having recently become acquainted with the social networking site, he noticed that Anders Fogh Rasmussen—his country's prime minister—was available as a friend. *That's odd*, he thought. He knew that there were countless fan pages dedicated to local and national leaders, but at that time, he'd never seen a politician who had his own personal page. Excited and intrigued, he sent a friend request to Rasmussen:

Mr. Rasmussen,

I know we're not friends. But, I teach social studies at a small school in Mariager, where I've worked for six years. I educate my students often on the very important role politicians play in the world. So I thought I'd reach out.

Sincerely,

Claus

To Claus's great surprise, his friend request was confirmed instantly, and he spent the following days in a miasma of exhilaration, thinking: *I have the best job in the world!* After all, there had been a long period in Denmark when some teachers were displeased with the working environment in the schools. And now that Claus and his colleagues were satisfied with not only their surroundings, but also their salaries, hours, and their amazing students, he knew he had to invite his new Facebook friend to see for himself.

The following week, Claus walked into his boss's office and declared, "I've become friends with our prime minister on Facebook, and I'd like to invite him to visit our school. Would that be okay?"

"You want to ask Anders Fogh Rasmussen to come here?" His boss laughed incredulously. "You might as well invite the pope."

"I'll go ahead, then," said Claus. "Thank you."

Back in his office, Claus prepared for his next move. *What does one write to the prime minister? What does one say to entice him?* Rasmussen was an athlete, he knew, and he even had a Facebook group with whom he went jogging once or twice a year. And Claus's school, Kridthuset, was on the banks of the Mariager Fjord, where each day he and his students would walk the one mile along the river. Perhaps he could invite Rasmussen to join his class on their daily jaunt. He wrote:

Mr. Rasmussen,

Hello, again.
To refresh your memory, I'm Claus
Drachmann, a teacher in Mariager. My school
is for special-needs kids, ranging from 6 to 15

years of age, and there are only 24 pupils in all.

I'd like to invite you to come for a jog next to the water with me and my students.

Sincerely,

Claus

Unlike the first time around, though, Claus received no response. In fact, he laughed at himself for even anticipating one. With a population of over 5 million, and 179 legislators in Denmark, if everybody sent a Facebook message to these politicians, they wouldn't have time to do anything but reply. Claus chalked it up to a good effort and left town to spend the school holiday with a friend.

Two months passed, and Claus had long since forgotten his message when—sitting on the front porch of his summer home—an unidentifiable number flashed on his cell phone.

"Is this Claus Drachmann?" a woman's voice asked.

"Yes it is. May I ask who is calling?"

"This is Anders Fogh Rasmussen's secretary," the woman revealed. "The prime minister is going to be giving a lecture at one of the gymnasiums in Jutland in September. It's only about twenty miles from your school, and his schedule is showing that he's got about an hour to spare. He'd like to spend it with your class."

"That's fantastic!" Claus replied at once.

"You'll have to take a number of security measures in advance," she warned. "Are you prepared to do that?"

"Of course I am!" Claus assured her. "Just say the word, and I'll do whatever it takes."

"Wonderful, then—we'll be in touch."

As soon as the line went dead, Claus shrieked with enthusiasm. The prime minister of Denmark had read his message, and, in a matter of months, was going to come to his school and spend an hour with his class!

The next day, Claus appeared in front of his boss again. "You know, he accepted the invitation," Claus delivered the news with a complacent grin from ear to ear.

"Who accepted the invitation?" His boss asked, looking up from a pile of paperwork.

"The prime minister."

"He's coming to our school?"

"Yup. He's going to walk with the kids along the bank of the Mariager Fjord for about an hour."

"Unbelievable."

"I know!" Claus's chest swelled with pride.

And, without delay, plans for the prime minister's visit were set in motion. It wasn't every day that politicians were spotted around Mariager. In truth, it wasn't *any* day, given that Rasmussen's offices were 185 miles away in Sealand. Thus, in light of the diminutive community's dearth of local star power, there were quite a few people who were more than a little anxious about welcoming their impending visitor.

Claus, on the other hand, was over the moon. He habitually spoke of democracy to his students, and had even shown them a video produced by the Danish Parliament, detailing their right to vote once they were older. The fact that they would be able to truly appreciate their guest was immeasurably satisfying.

Even the visit from Rasmussen's bodyguards and security brigade—a month in advance of the prime minister's arrival—was a delight for Claus's pupils, as they watched them check out everything from the classrooms to the kitchen to the toilets.

But it wasn't until the press started ringing that the drama unfolded. One morning, engaged in summer camp with his students, Claus received a call from a local journalist.

"I'd like to interview you and your students before the prime minister's visit," she said.

"That would be fine," Claus confirmed, thinking it would be a unique and special experience for his kids to talk to a newspaper reporter and to then see the article published the next day. "Why don't you come around and participate in our summer camp?"

Not long after that, television stations caught on, and Claus encouraged them to visit his school, cautioning, "My students have special gifts, and it's not that easy for them to have a lot of new people around them, with cameras. I've got some kids who would be very excited to talk to you and others who just want to meet the prime minister but would be too intimidated to speak with the press. So

HELLO, *Mr. Prime Minister*

could you please pay attention to the kids who would really like to tell you something? Then we'll all have a good experience."

Much to Claus's surprise, his request was granted, and the news spread like wildfire around his local community as residents eagerly awaited the big day.

On September 5, 2008—in response to Claus's Facebook message—Prime Minister Anders Fogh Rasmussen showed up at Claus's school, relaxed and happy, blending in with the other teachers and students as if he were one of them.

"Let's go for a walk," Rasmussen announced breezily, beckoning the kids to follow him. And as the brood regaled him with stories of their issues in the public school system, he listened to their declarations with intense interest: "What's good about this school? What are your benefits now?" he asked, smiling, since the answer was obvious.

For over an hour, the prime minister, Claus Drachmann, and twelve of his willing pupils walked along the river, chatting and laughing easily.

When it came time for Rasmussen to leave, the class gave him a special gift: a book that featured a collection of photos from the past hundred years of their school buildings and grounds. Their school had once served as the administrative office of a cement factory, located in the center of their town, which was home to the factory workers. Claus had inscribed the first page to his guest, and had also attached a card signed by the whole class.

It was a monumental moment for everyone.

"Thank you, Mr. Rasmussen, for visiting my school," Claus said, shaking the prime minister's hand. "I know you have a jog with your Facebook group later today in Aarhus, and since you came around to us, I'm going to participate in your run."

At four o'clock that afternoon, as Claus waited anxiously with the rest of Rasmussen's constituents outside his hotel, the prime minister appeared, ready for a three-mile jog in the forest.

Directly following the run, Rasmussen spoke to the Facebook group of eighty people, announcing, "I want to tell you a great story from this great day. I visited a little school in Northern Jutland, and I can see that the teacher is present. I had a very good experience, so thank you." Claus beamed and blushed simultaneously. It seemed inconceivable that the prime minister had acknowledged him—a former grocery store owner–cum–teacher.

Back at the office, Claus sat his desk, the frenetic buzz from his adventures still swirling around him. *This is the greatest day of my career*, he thought. *I have to thank the man who made this possible.* He logged on to Facebook again and wrote another note to another very important leader. This time, though, it wasn't a politician. It was the CEO of Facebook, Mark Zuckerberg. After relaying his story, Claus shared one final thought: *Mr. Zuckerberg, this tool you've created for connecting people is truly remarkable.*

And while he never heard back from the Facebook founder directly, he knows he got the message. Months later, Claus received an e-mail from a reporter at the *New York Times*, requesting an interview. Zuckerberg, he said, was the one who'd mentioned it to him.

On March 28, 2009, Claus's story appeared in the international newspaper, with the following quote from Mark Zuckerberg: "This represents a generational shift in technology . . . To me, what is interesting was that it was possible for a regular person to reach the prime minister and that that interaction happened."

To this day, Claus couldn't be more proud of his accomplishment: "Perhaps the most significant way I benefited from this experience was to see the trust I earned from my pupils. Relating to my kids is the foundation of everything I do, and it never would have been possible if not for Facebook," Claus reflects. "I try to teach my students that if they set a goal and are really determined to reach that goal, and do the best they can, they will achieve something. That's what our prime minister has always done."

On August 1, 2009, Anders Fogh Rasmussen assumed the post of Secretary General of NATO.

And on September 23, Claus Drachmann was named vice principal of Bredstrup-Pjedsted Primary School in Fredericia Municipality, Jutland, where he'll inspire 190 new students.

Photo Credit: **Bo Amstrup**

ELEVEN

TOUR DE *Source*

When Peter Shankman launched his boutique tech- and dot-com-centric public relations firm, The Geek Factory, in 1998—from his home office on the West Side of Manhattan—his goal was to take the world by storm. After all, with one cat and one computer as backup, how could he expect anything less?

The native New Yorker, thirteen-time marathon runner, triathlete, and licensed skydiver was used to taking chances, and accustomed to getting what he wanted through hard work and his own unique brand of perseverance. His new venture would surely follow suit.

By 2001, just three years after its inception, The Geek Factory was not only running smoothly, but was also one of the preeminent PR firms within its niche nationwide, boasting VIP clients like Snapple, Walt Disney, American Express, Harrah's Hotels, and even NASA. Things were going well for Peter. For the next six years, he continued to run his company with great success.

In addition to serving his long list of heavyweight clients, perhaps one of Peter's favorite aspects of his job as PR guru was to help reporters find sources, even if those sources didn't originate from his own firm's roster. Word spread, and reporters passed Peter's name along to their colleagues and friends. Before long, his phone was ringing multiple times a day as journalists across all media outlets grew dependent on his reliability.

One afternoon, sitting in his office, Peter received a call from a reporter with a particularly bizarre request. "I'm doing a story on Nigerian farming," he said. "I understand you know some soil experts."

"Yes, of course; that's how I organize all my friends," Peter joked, but he also realized that while he may not have had the answer to this specific request, there was someone out there who did. Furthermore, Peter knew he could do something to facilitate those connections.

So, in November of 2007, Peter decided to start a small Facebook group called, "If I can help a reporter out, I will." With thirty members to speak of—most of whom were Peter's friends—the group was established as an online portal where Peter could post the queries sent to him in order to assist journalists in finding sources for their stories.

Thirty members soon turned into fifty, which then doubled in size to one hundred, and before Peter knew what was happening, his grassroots experiment on Facebook had exploded into an 800-person group, which extended well beyond Peter's personal network.

Walking through a Duane Reade drugstore in Manhattan one morning (in search of ibuprofen for a broken rib) Peter received an unexpected call. It was the head of ProfNet, an online community of 14,000, also designed to connect reporters with sources.

"You're stealing our queries," declared the head of ProfNet matter-of-factly. "We're going to sue you."

"What?" Peter was confused. He was pretty sure he hadn't done anything wrong, much less engaged in thievery.

"We posted a query on Harry Potter and then you posted the same one."

"If a reporter sends me the same query as he sends you, how is that stealing your lead?" Peter questioned, and then, in the spirit of good faith, offered, "You want my Facebook members? I don't need them. I'm just doing this to be a nice guy. You know what? Buy me a steak and a martini and I'll give them all to you."

"Fine. We'll be in touch."

But a few months later, Peter still hadn't heard a peep from ProfNet, and, in the meantime, with 1,150 members, the group was dangerously close to outgrowing Facebook's 1,200-person group messaging capacity. *I can do this on my own*, he thought, and called his friend Adam, a computer programmer, to see what it would involve to start his own website.

"How long will it take to set this up?" Peter inquired, detailing his vision—a simple online repository to link reporters with legitimate sources.

"I can do it overnight," Adam replied.

And in March of 2008, Peter sent out the first Help a Reporter Out (HARO) query from his hotel room in Los Angeles, and the website, helpareporter.com, was born.

The welcome page of Peter's Facebook group now read:

Hey everyone!

Short story: We've outgrown Facebook! This is a good thing!

It means our little experiment here in social media and PR is working!

This makes me happy. :)

But, we're getting bigger, and we've outgrown our playpen!

So before Facebook cuts off messaging access, we're going to move.

Welcome to Help a Reporter Out, Volume 2. The site's been built to be as simple as this one: Simply enter your name/company/ e-mail, and you'll get reporter requests sent to you via e-mail, usually immediately after a reporter sends them to me.

It's simple, it's STILL FREE, and it's no SPAM. It's a double-opt-in list, with an automatic opt-out if you ever decide to leave us. Couldn't be simpler, and yes, I'm still doing this because it's good karma.

Do me one favor, though—TELL YOUR FRIENDS. I'd kind of like for this to grow. It's a simple idea, and one that can really help not only reporters, but all of us, as well! The bigger it gets, the better chance we have to make sure that reporters get the sources they need. The more they get the sources they need, the more likely they are to tell other journalists, which in the end, gives you more chances to get yourself, your clients, or your company some good press!

So tell your friends. Tell your reporters! Blog about it! Link to the site! Put it in newsletters! Speak of it when you're sitting in thy house! (Hee.)

Anyhow—thanks for being a part of this. You've helped this little experiment grow, and I can't wait for the growth to continue.

Sign up, help a reporter, help yourself, and have some fun.

Blue skies,

Peter Shankman

By July, Peter's query list had grown from one to 1,200 per week, and two new features had been added to his thrice-daily HARO e-mails—a short blurb about a HARO "family member" (paying sponsor), and an update from Peter as to his whereabouts at any given moment.

All of a sudden the entrepreneur, public relations whiz, and social media sage realized he had a second full-time job, and it was time to make a choice—The Geek Factory or HARO. His gut was rallying for the latter.

And, one year post-inception, it turns out Peter's gut was right. HARO grossed over a million dollars in revenue in 2009, and currently boasts close to 100,000 members worldwide. He's got a staff of four, stationed in New York City, White Plains, Philadelphia, and Arizona. And, beyond his nearly 100,000 followers, Peter estimates that—through word of mouth—his reach is over twice that number. Not to mention that his speaking fees have gone through the roof.

Now the largest free source repository in the world, with an 85 percent open read on its e-mails, HARO's tagline— "Everyone Is an Expert at Something"—has proven true in more ways than one. But, despite the company's virtual overnight success, Peter Shankman is far from content. His new goal: "Grow, grow, and grow some more."

And if you do decide to join the ever-expanding HARO family, here's what you'll find on their website today:

Welcome to Help a Reporter Out™!

This list was originally conceived on Facebook, but since Facebook caps group messages at 1,200 people, this is the next incarnation.

Each day, you'll receive up to three e-mails, each with anywhere from 15 to 30 queries per e-mail. They'll all be labeled with [shankman.com] in the subject line, for easy filtering. If you see a query you can answer, go for it! HelpAReporter.com really is that simple.

I built this list because a lot of my friends are reporters, and they call me all the time for sources. Rather than go through my contact lists each time, I figured I could push the requests out to people who actually have something to say.

These requests only come from reporters directly to me. I never take queries from that other service, I never SPAM, and I'm not going to do anything with your e-mail other than send you these reporter requests when they arrive in my in-box.

So a few things about this list: First off, yes, it's free. It takes me a few minutes each day to do this, and the good karma is immeasurable. So I'm not charging. If you really feel like sending me a donation or something, why not just send a few bucks to an animal hospital or animal rescue society somewhere? Some good places are Best Friends Animal Sanctuary or The National Search Dog Foundation. That'll keep the good karma flowing.

Next—this is really the only thing I ask: By joining this list, just promise me and yourself that you'll ask yourself before you send a response: Is this response really on target? Is this response really going to help the journalist, or is this just a BS way for me to get my client in front of the reporter? If you have to think for more than three seconds, chances are you shouldn't send the response.

In the end, we could probably all stand to do this a bit more, huh?

That's it. No other rules.

Thanks for being here, and thanks for using Help a Reporter Out!

Blue skies!
Peter Shankman

As for Peter, well, he's still taking the world by storm. And he definitely appreciates the value of a clever idea spiked with a healthy dose of risk: "Everyone likes to be a hero. When you see a query that works for you or for a friend, the first thing you do is forward it. Your friend gets quoted in the *New York Times,* and there you go. You can't be more of a hero than that."

Peter adds, "I started HARO on Facebook merely as a means of helping my friends. There are thousands of groups formed on Facebook every day. But, you can't make something viral. You can, however, make something good. And that's what we've done. We've created something that allows people to say, 'Hey, I see why this is beneficial. I want to use this. I want to send this to my friends.' The viral part will take care of itself. I think I've proven that. All I can tell you is that HARO completely changed my life, which was just about the last thing I expected to happen from an innocuous Facebook group."

TWELVE

MAGIC *Touch*

*B*arbara Fischkin remembers it like it was yesterday—ringing in the Chinese New Year in Hong Kong with her husband, Jim, and their sons, Daniel and Jack, whose stirring rendition of "Twinkle, Twinkle, Little Star" in Cantonese stole the show.

That was nearly twenty years ago. It was also the last time Daniel spoke.

Born in September 1987, in Mexico City—where Barbara, an author and journalist, and Jim, a Pulitzer Prize–winning former investigative editor and reporter, were foreign correspondents—Daniel was just like any other baby. He was happy and healthy. His Apgar score was normal, and Barbara and Jim considered themselves to be very lucky.

A year and a half later, the family of three relocated to Hong Kong, and, in 1990, welcomed their newest addition, son Jack. All was right with the world.

A few months passed, and Daniel—who'd just turned three and had a history of ear infections—came down with a 106-degree fever and severe dehydration. He wound up in the hospital, and Barbara and Jim remained stalwart at his side. It was an unwelcome scare, certainly, but nothing life-threatening, and Daniel was released with a clean bill of health. Or so they thought.

Almost immediately, Barbara and Jim began to detect changes in their formerly extroverted child. At first, he seemed uninterested in playing with the other kids at his Montessori school in Hong Kong. Then came an aberrant habit—Daniel started chewing his shirt. And, before long, the boy who'd once spoken fluent English and had learned words and phrases in Spanish, Cantonese, and Tagalog—the national language in the Philippines—lost the ability to communicate altogether.

Was Daniel reacting to suddenly having a new brother and no longer being an only child? Was it the prospect of moving from Hong Kong back to the United States? Barbara and Jim had questions, but no answers. All they knew was that their happy-go-lucky three-year-old had practically mutated, in the course of six months, into someone who was acutely autistic. It was as if one child had disappeared and another had taken his place—one that was entirely unrecognizable to his loved ones.

Daniel's parents were beside themselves with grief, knowing they might never be able to reclaim the young, vibrant boy they were once so intimately acquainted with. But, they also knew that marinating in their sorrow would help neither them nor Daniel. So Barbara and Jim decided to take action.

They read books, articles, medical studies—anything they could get their hands on—that might shed even the dimmest light on Daniel's condition. The Yale Child Study Center called it "Child Disintegrative Disorder," the worst kind of autism, submitting that children who suffered from it would be institutionalized by the time they were ten years old.

Not Daniel, they told themselves, and vowed to keep him at home, in their doting family fold, for as long as they could.

Pursuing further research, Barbara discovered a then-controversial technique, dubbed "Facilitated Communication," for kids experiencing sensory difficulties. If Daniel couldn't speak, perhaps, Barbara reasoned, this would be an alternate method of social interaction. And while most school programs had yet to accept it, she didn't let that stand in her way. She practiced with Daniel, resting her hand lightly on top of his to provide a reverse pressure that would allow him to move his own hand—the idea being that, by doing so, he might be able to type on a keyboard one day.

For the next decade, Barbara worked tirelessly with Daniel to improve this skill, employing all manner of computer programs designed for autistic individuals, and often being bitten by her son—in moments of frustration—throughout the process. But there was nothing that enabled Daniel to type independently or engaged him enough to remain at the keyboard for any length of time.

After an arduous transition through puberty, at the age of fifteen, it was decided that Daniel would have to move to a group home. Although it wasn't what they wanted, Barbara and Jim added their eldest son's name to an emergency list, with no idea when a spot would become available.

Over the course of the following five years, at home, Daniel worked assiduously with a speech therapist. When he turned nineteen, he began to learn PROMPT therapy, a systematic means of linking motor skills to speech production by using hands-on tactile indicators. Through this, he was able to process a few familiar words, such as "mom" and "hi," which he hadn't been able to do since his regression over fifteen years earlier. Daniel also had some success with the Picture Exchange Communication System (PECS), a method where either Barbara or the speech therapist made laminated squares of pictures or words and Daniel would hand them to people as a form of letting them know what he wanted.

Despite his progress, though, at the age of twenty-one, he still tested like a nonverbal three-year-old, and while he was clearly very bright, a one-on-one aide was required at all times. Barbara felt at a loss. *Is there nothing out there that will ever help Daniel?* she agonized.

This hopeless feeling persisted until the fall of 2008, when a journalist friend sent her an e-mail saying, "Hey, I can't get on your wall."

"What's a wall?" Barbara wrote back.

"Facebook!" she replied.

Barbara, who'd joined the social networking site, and had—clearly—forgotten all about it, logged on. Her first reaction was, *Wow! This looks cool!*

And then it occurred to her. Facebook was not only cool, but it amalgamated two senses—touch and sight. *I wonder if Daniel would like this,* she mused.

Without hesitation, Barbara introduced Daniel to her latest, greatest "discovery," and instantly he started laughing. He'd laughed before, sure, but rarely when typing. That had typically been a very serious experience for Daniel, one that he did not delight in. But, beyond laughter, Barbara saw recognition. And with a little encouragement, she soon found that Daniel responded better to Facebook than to any other communication-typing program he'd ever tried, even those designed by educational scholars. No other program so artfully combined photos with the option for brevity.

Together, mother and son set up Daniel's profile and, before long, his camp counselors were sending friend requests and posting photos of his happiest moments from the previous summer—photos that resonated with Daniel and rescued him from the winter doldrums.

Even though he couldn't type independently, Daniel was able to use a laptop mouse to click and accept new friends, which—for the first time—afforded him a significant sense of empowerment.

Barbara would say, "Here is somebody who is requesting to be your friend," pointing with the mouse. And Daniel would left-click by himself. It was, quite obviously, an extraordinary turn of events.

A few weeks later, overjoyed by her son's progress, Barbara received a message via Facebook from a woman named Chou Chou Scantlin, who confided:

 I'm fifty-five years old. I don't share this with many people, but I suffer from high-functioning autism, and I love Facebook! Would you mind if I "friend" your son Daniel?

As part of a lifelong quest to understand her condition, one day Chou Chou—a showgirl, powerhouse singer, and former Shakespearean actress, who'd been struggling, mostly in private, with a form of the very same autism that Daniel had been living with for two decades—had searched "Facebook for Autistics" and had found a blog Barbara had written about Daniel. It mentioned that he had joined Facebook, and that the combination of text and photographs, representing many people he already knew, seemed to make it easier for him to focus and communicate, even without speech.

Chou Chou, who was able to perform, in part, because she saw light instead of the members of her audiences, corresponded with Barbara again about her own similar reaction:

In a social situation, or just being out in the world, there is much torturous confusion. E-mailing is faceless but not in a good or inviting way. It is like talking to someone who's in a dark cave. The phone is no good, because, well, the expressions seem all wrong on both ends. Then came Facebook. I can see my friends' faces, which I adore, but there is no getting overwhelmed or confused by their expressions, movements, voices, or idiosyncrasies. It is so simple and light and charming, and

> since people take the time to connect, it
> takes away any fear that you are bothering
> them. As I read the postings on the other
> walls, the mystery of socializing unfolds to
> me in a way I have never understood.

Touched by her newfound friend's sincerity, Barbara asked Jim, with a knowing smile on her face, "Do you think Daniel would like to be friends with a beautiful fifty-five-year-old showgirl?"

Jim returned her smile and replied, "Don't I get first dibs?"

"She keeps her clothes on," Barbara laughed.

"Too bad," he countered, still grinning.

Humor aside, Barbara and Jim decided the connection would not only help Daniel but also bolster his self-esteem. From that point on, Daniel and Chou Chou began to communicate back and forth, writing on each other's walls. And when Barbara didn't understand a behavior her son was exhibiting, she had a wonderful resource in Chou Chou.

These days, Daniel, who clicks to make friends on his own but still needs help with his motor functions, expresses his thoughts often on his Facebook profile, writing:

i like people but u really need understand autism i dont show a lot but i feel much and want many many friends.

Barbara, relieved to have found an outlet that's not only age-appropriate for her son, but so much more fun than sitting around typing aimlessly, can hardly believe Daniel's enthusiasm. As soon as she takes out his laptop, an ear-to-ear grin spreads across his face. And when she introduces him to new people, she says, "Daniel is on Facebook. You can become his friend," which—invariably—they do.

Daniel communicates with his father, brother, uncle, cousins, and even grandfather on Facebook. He's also a member of a Facebook group for individuals with autism who type more articulately than they speak.

Seven years after his name was added to the state list, Daniel moved into a temporary group home thirty minutes from his family's house on Long Island. Several months later, he moved again, to a beautiful home renovated by the Association for the Help of Retarded Children in Nassau County, an organization that was started for the mentally retarded and now also serves many clients with autism. Naturally, Daniel enjoys overnight visits with his parents, who will continue to help him correspond with his 330-plus Facebook friends in the manner to which he's become accustomed.

In the meantime, Barbara and Jim will aggressively pursue the latest, cutting-edge autism research with Autism Associates of New York, who are examining the immune system as opposed to the brain, and looking closely at heavy-metal and environmental toxicity. They will study Daniel's immune system, Barbara's immune system, and Jim's immune system, in order to piece together a cohesive family profile, which they hope will provide some of the answers they've been searching for, for so long: Did Daniel have some sort of genetic susceptibility to environmental toxins that caused his drastic transformation? Was it a vaccine? Mercury or lead poisoning?

Barbara, who's currently writing a nonfiction book, tentatively titled *Dan the Man and His Generation*, examining the big picture of adult autism and chronicling her son's entrance into the adult world while battling—and sometimes reveling in—the condition, says:

There are very few miracles with autism, but there are many slow processes and slow kinds of therapies and interventions that work very well. Facebook is one of these nonmedical therapies. There's been a fortune spent and a fortune made on computer programs for kids with autism, and I haven't found any that's worked as well for Daniel and has kept him occupied for as long as Facebook does.

It's changing his life by making him feel part of what the mainstream does.

She adds, "Let's just say Daniel will remain on Facebook for as long as he wants . . . and five years from now, my expectation is that he'll be doing it with no help at all. We don't know if his condition is forever. We don't know if anything is forever. But as soon as you give up hope, that's when hope dies."

Photo Credit: **Christopher Zach**

KITTY IN THE *City*

*J*t was January of 2006 when Nicole and Shane Meide returned from their ten-day honeymoon in the Dominican Republic, ready to start off the New Year and their new marriage with an important addition to their family.

With three children already in their brood—a seven-year-old daughter from Nicole's previous relationship, and a nine-year-old daughter and three-year-old son from Shane's—they weren't quite ready for a baby, but a cat sounded like a good plan. And with no other pets, aside from fish, to speak of, the Meides decided an animal would not only provide hours of fun for their clan of five, but also teach the kids important lessons about responsibility. Since a cat would not be as high-maintenance as a dog, it seemed like a smart place to start.

Determined not to buy a cat from a breeder when there were so many homeless felines out there, Nicole and Shane headed to the local Humane Society, where they'd been casually browsing for about a year. As they looked around from one sweet face to the next, Shane noticed an enormous, fluffy Maine coon in one of the cages that appeared to weigh about twenty pounds. Maine coons, they were told, were one of the oldest natural breeds in North America, known for their brawny bone structure, flowing coat, keen intelligence, and mild personalities. Amber, the woman at the Humane Society, told them he was about three years old, though they didn't know his exact birthday, and that he was particularly unique because he had six digits on each paw. For $150 he could be all theirs.

As Shane folded the cat into his arms, the animal began to purr contentedly, as if to say, "Take me home with you."

"Honey, we have to rescue this cat," Shane said. He was sold, and turned to his wife for approval.

"You're absolutely right," Nicole agreed wholeheartedly, thinking that their children would surely love the lively kitty as much as they already did.

And, with that, the Meides handed over the $150 and bundled their new cat—whom they'd decided to name Bob—into the car and drove him back to their home in East Bethel, Minnesota.

But when Bob got home, his personality shifted. The spirited kitty they'd encountered at the Humane Society slept for two days straight, and when he awoke, didn't want anything to do with anyone—with the exception of Nicole, as time went on.

Bob swiftly became solely Nicole's cat, keeping his distance from Shane and even the children. And he always— always—did things on his own terms. When Nicole would call him, Bob would come, but not all the way. He'd stop about a foot short of her, indicating that if she wanted to pet him, it would have to be from a distance. If anyone other than Nicole so much as tried to stroke his downy mane, they would often get bitten. The Meides even contemplated hanging a sign that said: BEWARE OF CAT!

As Bob loitered around the house day in and day out, lazy and rotund, uninterested in human contact, Nicole and Shane often wondered what had happened to the amiable kitty they'd first met at the Humane Society. Sure, he'd step outside on the rare occasion, even though the porch door was always left open for him, but that was the extent of Bob's adventures and, after a year and a half, the Meide family became accustomed to their lovable but unloving cat.

Until May of 2007, that is, when Bob surprised everyone.

Nicole and Shane came downstairs in the morning, waiting for Bob to announce his appetite. After all, he was typically quiet until feeding time, when he'd purr loudly, almost like a baby crying for its morning meal. But on this morning, he was nowhere to be found. Nicole and Shane searched the house frantically for their beloved Bob, high and low, under every bed, behind every cabinet, and around every corner; they even peeked out the sliding door to the back porch, which they'd left open, as always, overnight. He wasn't there. It soon became clear to Nicole and Shane that Bob had broken his usual pattern of indolence; he had obviously escaped in the early morning hours. Immediately, they canvassed the neighborhood, screaming Bob's name from the car windows.

"What if someone saw him on the street and took him?" Nicole asked Shane, panic shrouding her face. "He's so beautiful, and he's a purebred."

"Don't worry; we'll find him." Shane reassured her even though his own optimism was beginning to dwindle, as their search crept up in hours and down in hope.

"At least it's warm out so he won't freeze," Nicole said, taking solace in the temperate, 70-degree May weather, a rare balmy time of year in Minnesota. And then she had a thought: "Let's go home and get Bob's favorite cat food. Maybe we can lure him with that."

"Good idea," Shane replied, relieved to have a new plan that might bring Bob back to them.

No such luck. The rest of the day, and the days following that, were spent going from house to house, knocking on every door, with color photos of Bob that Nicole had printed off her computer. She'd also made flyers that they posted around the neighborhood for everyone to see.

Three days later, still on their mission to track down Bob, Nicole knocked on the door of an elderly couple a few houses down from theirs.

"Hello, I'm Nicole Meide, and I live down the street. I'm wondering if you've seen my cat, Bob?" She held up the photo and smiled hopefully.

"Why, yes, we have," they reported, happy to be of help to the lovely young lady on their doorstep. "We saw him under the vacant house across the road—you know the one."

She did. She'd even circled that very house looking for Bob, calling out his name. *Why hadn't he responded to her desperate pleas?* Nicole thanked the elderly couple and drove directly to the vacant house once again.

She crept along the side of the house and knelt down to check underneath. There was Bob, looking right back at her. Nicole was thrilled, calling to her kitty, and reaching her arm as far toward him as she could, beckoning him to come toward her. But Bob wouldn't budge.

Frustrated, Nicole sped back to her house to get his favorite food. She hadn't had a chance to use it the first time, but now that she knew where Bob was hiding out, this would surely be the answer. She was beyond thankful that he was unharmed, and anxious to surprise Shane with the fantastic news!

Back at the vacant house, Nicole knelt down once again, and there was Bob, right where she'd left him. She breathed a sigh of relief and presented him with the food.

"Come on, Bob. Come to Mommy. You know you want some," she encouraged.

Bob put one paw in front of him and then promptly ran in the opposite direction, leaving Nicole not only thwarted but bemused.

"Maybe he just didn't like us," Nicole cried to Shane later that night. "Maybe he just wants to be an alley cat." She knew Bob could hold his own against other animals, resembling a raccoon himself, but what about other people? What if he came across someone who didn't like cats, and they brought him to the pound?

Every single day that followed, Nicole and Shane returned to the vacant house, each time with a small glimmer of hope that Bob had changed his mind and wanted to come home. The Meides even called the Humane Society, where they'd first found Bob, remembering that the society had microchips inserted in all of their animals, in the event that they got lost or ran away. However, they were informed that said chips were only useful if someone brought Bob back to them, in which case they'd be able to use the chip to figure out who he belonged to. It was not, as they'd hoped, a means of tracking Bob's specific whereabouts.

Alas, Nicole and Shane resigned themselves to never seeing Bob again, and, over a year later, in June of 2008, they moved sixty miles away to Big Lake, Minnesota. They welcomed three new additions to their growing tribe—a baby girl, a new Ragdoll kitten, and a boxer puppy. Despite their joy in their expanding family, however, nothing could fill the void left by Bob's absence.

Nearly ten months later, Nicole was sitting at her computer at home when she came across some old photos of Bob. She showed them to Shane.

"I really miss him," she said, her eyes welling with fresh tears.

"Me too," he agreed. There was nothing more to say.

A few days later, back at her computer, Nicole received an invitation from her stepdaughter's mother to join Facebook. She and Shane had resisted joining the social networking site up to that point, convinced it was more for single people looking for love, and besides, they had little time for frivolous activities with their family of four kids and two animals to take care of. But, given the circumstances surrounding the invitation, Nicole felt compelled to sign up, and Shane was soon to follow.

The next night, around 8 P.M., Nicole—slightly more tech-savvy than her husband—was helping Shane create his own page, when a message came into his in-box. Figuring it was a "Welcome to Facebook" kind of thing, she clicked on it and her mouth fell open.

"Shane, get over here. You have to read this!" She jolted with excitement.

Amber, the woman whom they'd purchased Bob from at the Humane Society, had contacted Shane, saying, "We think we found your cat."

Since the Meides hadn't updated Bob's microchip information when they moved, convinced that he was gone for good, Amber had had no way of finding them. They'd changed their cell phone numbers too, and even though she'd attempted to locate them via the White Pages and by Googling them online, nothing had worked. Finally, she'd thought, *What the heck; I'll try a shot in the dark and see if they're on Facebook.* If it had been only one day earlier, Amber would have come up empty again.

Jumping up and down and crying in unison, Shane and Nicole could hardly believe the serendipity. Immediately, they messaged her back, even though she wasn't in the office, and were told they could come and retrieve Bob anytime after noon the following day, when the Humane Society opened. Since they were nearly an hour away, Shane would pick Bob up on his way home from work at 4 P.M. They could hardly wait the twenty hours, every passing minute amounting to a lifetime.

When the clock struck noon the next day, Nicole called Amber to thank her and to alert her to Shane's impending arrival.

"How did you find him?" she asked, curiosity finally replacing sheer exhilaration. Amber informed Nicole that their old neighbors, who hadn't put two and two together after such an extended period of time, had been feeding Bob for about six months. They could no longer afford to take care of him, so they'd brought him to the Humane Society. There, they'd identified Bob from his microchip, but had been unable to locate the Meides. Amber revealed that they'd never connected a pet with its owner through Facebook before, so it hadn't been their first instinct.

"We just can't thank you enough," Nicole repeated. "You have the most wonderful job in the world." Five hours later—and two years after his escape—Shane brought Bob home to the waiting arms of Nicole and their kids. Everyone was overjoyed, including Bob, who purred more vociferously than ever.

These days, Bob is loving life in his new house in Big Lake, with an entirely different personality. "He's completely affectionate now," says Nicole. "He sleeps with our children in their beds, which was unheard of before."

And even though Bob can occasionally be found gazing out the window with a wistful glint in his eyes, he's happy right where he is—safe at home, surrounded by his family.

FOURTEEN

A MILLION *Voices*

*I*t was 1966 in Colombia when Manuel Marulanda Vélez, along with other members of the country's Communist Party, established a new guerrilla group based on Marxist ideology.

The rebel movement, FARC (Fuerzas Armadas Revolucionarias de Colombia, or Revolutionary Armed Forces of Colombia), was initiated by Marulanda to fight against the government, claiming equal opportunity and an equitable distribution of wealth.

Over the following two decades, FARC vigorously staged raids against government forces while kidnapping wealthy Colombians and holding them for ransom. While the group claimed to be defending the citizens of Colombia, it was evident to the country's constituents that their actions belied their intent. Rapidly, they involved themselves in all manner of terrorist activity—bombing and attacking towns and cities, indiscriminately murdering innocent Colombians, and hijacking airplanes. After the extinction of the major drug cartels, FARC also took control of the illegal narcotics business, eventually evolving into the worldwide leaders of cocaine and heroin production.

There was little anyone could do to stop them—until 2002, when president Álvaro Uribe conceived a program called "Democratic Security," which diminished and controlled FARC's terrorist pursuits. But, despite this long-sought-after victory against FARC, 700 people still remained in captivity, some for over ten years, and FARC used these hostages as merchant goods to negotiate political representation.

President Uribe knew he needed assistance, and thus appointed Venezuelan president Hugo Chávez to act as a mediator with the rebel group. Chávez operated quickly and effectively, announcing in early December of 2007 that, thanks to his arbitration, FARC had agreed to liberate three kidnapped citizens: Clara Rojas, her young son Emmanuel (who had been born in captivity), and Consuelo González.

Three weeks passed as the entire country awaited the liberation of the three kidnap victims with enthused expectancy. There was no word from either camp; FARC remained silent, as did President Chávez.

On December 31, President Uribe addressed the nation, informing them that an investigation had exposed the fact that FARC was no longer in possession of Emmanuel. They'd abandoned him in a small clinic in San José del Guaviare, and—in light of this development—FARC refused to fulfill their promise of liberation.

President Uribe's announcement was not received well, and was the catalyst for unprecedented indignation and anger among all Colombian citizens, who, once again, felt deceived and assaulted by the guerrilla group. Burdened with uncertainty and fear, the people of Colombia were rendered hopeless. If two world leaders had failed to negotiate with FARC, how could anyone hope to succeed?

Enter Oscar Morales Guevara, a thirty-year-old engineer from Barranquilla with an idea. He'd been a member of Facebook for about a year, and had devoted several hours a day to participating in discussion boards of groups related to Colombian politics. Oscar knew that the growing social network had been met with strong approval when introduced to his country, and, since that time, it had become very common for Colombian users to join groups and take part in the activism generated by them.

"Wouldn't Facebook be the perfect arena for proposing a campaign against FARC?" he asked his family, who agreed unconditionally that the cry for protest was in the air—not only in their home, but in the homes of all Colombians, on the streets, and in offices. It was palpable.

"I don't want to fall into the cliché of launching a group with a title, logo, and description, with the sole purpose of recruiting members to feed my ego," he explained. "I want this group to stand out and to surpass the hundreds of groups that have no ideology or pursue shallow purposes."

His family supported his agenda, and Oscar took this as a sign that he must move forward with his plan. So, on January 4, 2008, he created a Facebook group called "One Million Voices Against FARC," spending several hours late into the night designing the logo and writing copy for the page. The logo, with a vertical Colombian flag as its backdrop, presented this message:

No more kidnapping. No more lies. No more death. No more FARC.

Oscar chose his words carefully, cognizant that there was already a handful of successful groups like his with over 100,000 members. But his ambitions proved even greater. He opted for "million" instead of "thousand," and "voices" rather than "people," describing FARC's terrorist actions, and including a desperate plea to all Colombians to join together against this guerrilla faction.

Twelve hours later, the group boasted 1,500 members. After twenty-four hours, it had reached 4,000, and within two days, it had grown to 9,000. Simultaneously, the group's discussion board boiled with hundreds of topics and heated messages.

This success notwithstanding, there was still a remarkable contrast in member count when compared to established Facebook groups with the same theme. Despite invitations and news-feed posts, Oscar simply couldn't attract enough people. The group was surely an instrument to express the frustration, anger, and disappointment alive among Colombian people, but that wasn't enough for Oscar. He searched his mind for an alternative—some other way he could use the Facebook group to effect change.

"What if I could use the strength and rapid growth of this movement to go out to the streets and form a real protest?" he discussed with his family, who encouraged his new objective.

Inspired by their support, he created an event on the group's Facebook page, called "National March Against FARC." One month, he reasoned, would be enough time to organize the march. He set the date for February 4, 2008, and invited people to flood the streets of Colombia in a manifestation against FARC. It would take place at noon in Colombia.

Oscar's hope was that the response would be great, but there was no way he could anticipate the overwhelming reaction from people across the globe. Immediately, Colombians who lived outside the country replicated the march in their own cities and countries abroad, forcing Oscar to change the event's title to "Worldwide Mobilization Against FARC."

What happened next was an unprecedented domino effect. Oscar and his volunteers designed a press communication strategy that allowed them to work together from remote locations. They corresponded via Facebook, e-mail, and Skype, sharing documents and building a database with the information of all coordinators, while new ones were recruited day by day. They also crafted a functions manual, with a list of tasks to be performed in each city in order for the marches to work.

On January 9, just five days after the group's creation, and two days after the creation of the international march, "One Million Voices Against FARC" had 40,000 members and volunteer coordinators in nearly forty cities worldwide.

That same day, Oscar went public with their press communications via a newly designed website, and published the story of the Facebook group's inception and its unparalleled success. Having compiled a database with over 100 e-mail addresses from journalists, news directors, newspaper editors, opinion leaders, and TV-show hosts, their cell phones began ringing within hours of going live. Everyone Oscar spoke to was intrigued by the Facebook boom. They couldn't believe that such a staunch political protest had been bred from a social networking site.

Daily, Oscar and his volunteers were being interviewed on the radio and TV, expounding on the facts of their grassroots effort on Facebook, and providing details on the upcoming marches. As the word spread around Colombia and throughout the world, Oscar began meeting with mayors and police chiefs to obtain the necessary permits that would allow the marches to take place. He also received hefty donations from global industries, including publicity services, infrastructure, audio, T-shirts, and other goods.

On January 17, the newspaper *El Tiempo* dedicated their editorial to Oscar's group, and invited everyone, on their behalf, to join the "Worldwide Mobilization Against FARC." All of a sudden, Oscar's dreams were transforming into reality, as people around the world marveled at the fact that the mobilization had been envisaged and organized by a bunch of ordinary, young folks with no prior experience in grassroots movements. Like Oscar, most of the participants were in their thirties, and their resources were limited.

CNN, along with other media in the United States, Spain, France, Brazil, Venezuela, Argentina, Mexico, Italy, and various South American countries, followed the developments every day. RCN and CARACOL, the most influential television stations in Colombia, also gave Oscar their full support—covering the evolution of the Facebook group and the preparations for the marches. Vendors everywhere were selling T-shirts emblazoned with the official logo of the group: NO MAS FARC.

With the historic day just one week away, all of Oscar's organizers concentrated on the logistics in their own cities, attending meetings with high-level authorities in order to guarantee the security and health of the marchers. They were also held accountable for the tasks of coordinating traffic, closing off streets, and making sure firemen, paramedics, and health personnel were on hand. The excitement in the air was tangible as Oscar and his team worked feverishly to set everything in motion.

And then the day arrived—February 4, 2008. A day that, unbeknownst to Oscar, would be forever etched in the history of his country as the greatest mobilization of all time. Twelve million people from around the world took to the streets. More than 200 cities in 40 different countries were flooded with marchers. Then-senator Hillary Clinton announced it was the largest demonstration ever held against any terrorist organization.

In July 2008, the Colombian Armed Forces rescued Ingrid Betancourt, three American citizens, and eleven soldiers from FARC. One of these soldiers, along with Ingrid, incited a second march on July 20, with over 15 million participants—once again unleashing "One Million Voices Against FARC" onto the international scene.

Four days later, with the strength of 418,000 members behind him, Oscar brought to fruition his latest achievement: the One Million Voices Foundation, which will work toward the defense of human rights, to increase international pressure against kidnapping, and to help demobilize individuals taken hostage by these guerrilla groups.

"Our goals are ambitious," Oscar acknowledges. "But with the help of many, we will continue to lead the way in the Great Worldwide Mobilization Against FARC."

FIFTEEN

HEALING *Hearts*

When Amy Eldridge adopted a little girl from China in the year 2000, there was only one thing missing: She wasn't able to visit the orphanage where her daughter had been living, and it left her feeling disappointed, even a bit anxious.

Amy knew that she needed to see her sweet baby's former home, but since she'd been one of the first people to adopt from that particular orphanage, and a foreigner had yet to set foot inside, she wasn't permitted. For three years, Amy continued to pursue her goal, ultimately befriending an English-speaking Chinese college student whose mother volunteered at the orphanage and was able to facilitate a tour.

In the spring of 2003, Amy headed back to China to finally see with her own eyes the place where her daughter had lived. As she explored the space with the orphanage doctor and played with some of the kids, she couldn't help but notice a young boy in one of the beds who was—alarmingly—blue in the face.

"What's wrong with him?" Amy asked, motioning to the obviously ill child.

"He has severe heart disease," the doctor replied.

"When will his surgery be?" Amy knelt down to stroke the poor boy's arm.

"There isn't going to be one," the doctor disclosed, tilting his eyes downward despondently. "We don't have the money."

Amy shook her head at the injustice. She then met three other children, suffering the same affliction, who would not be able to have their heart maladies healed. One was a three-year-old girl who couldn't even walk across the room without stopping to kneel frequently, in order to catch her breath.

Back home in Oklahoma, Amy couldn't shake the images of the terminally ill children in the orphanage. As a mother of six, herself—five biological children in addition to her adopted daughter—and one of only a few people in the United States who knew these children even existed in such dire circumstances, she was determined to do something.

Amy's first step was to send an e-mail to friends and family, asking for people to help—which they did. Flooded with donations and letters of support, she was able to heal all four of the orphanage's children in need. *I can't stop now*, Amy thought. *There are always going to be more children who require medical attention.*

So, with her newfound connections in China, Amy, along with five of her friends—all adoptive parents— founded Love Without Boundaries in August of the same year. Their one and only goal was to help kids.

Initially conceived as a medical program, Love Without Boundaries rapidly expanded, spreading its wings into foster care and education, training teachers to work with children ranging in age from two to twenty, who weren't able to thrive in the public school system.

And in 2006, Amy adopted her second child from China— a little boy. Everything was running smoothly with Love Without Boundaries, and Amy couldn't have been prouder to add a seventh child to her ever-expanding brood.

Unfortunately, on New Year's Eve of 2007, the Love Without Boundaries website was hacked, rendering it impossible for any donations to be received during the typically abundant holiday season. Amy and her colleagues were mortified, and their misfortune was laden with both technical and emotional distress. Love Without Boundaries existed and was funded entirely online, their rationale being that if volunteers worked remotely across the country, rather than spending money on an office and administrative fees, they could give all of their contributions to the children—the ones who needed it most.

As Amy wracked her brain to find a solution, she recalled an e-mail a friend had sent her about a Facebook Charity Challenge. She hadn't paid it much attention. After all, as a mother to seven, she hardly had time to kill on social networking sites. But faced with this alternate method of raising money, Amy decided to at least set up a Facebook page to replace their existing website until they could get it back up and running.

Still, the organization didn't jump into the challenge, which was already under way. How could they compete with the substantially larger organizations like the American Cancer Society or the Red Cross, especially when they were entering the game at such a late stage?

"If we don't at least try, we'll never know what could have been," one of the volunteers in China reminded Amy. And Amy knew she was right. They had to throw their hat into the ring, even if it was the smallest cap in the bunch.

With their website still nonfunctioning, Amy and her volunteers rallied around their new objective with renewed vigor and a commitment to do everything they could to raise money for the orphans in China—even if they had no chance of winning the Facebook challenge.

In researching the challenge, Amy realized that—in addition to the $50,000 grand prize—there was also $1,000 awarded daily to whichever charity brought in the most money on any given day. "Let's win some of those," Amy said, cheering on her troops. "If we can win just a couple, we could heal a child."

Before long, though, Amy realized that Love Without Boundaries was not only doing well, they were moving up in the contest rankings at lightning speed. So they decided to re-strategize, telling everyone they knew that since the grand prize was $50,000 and heart surgery costs about $5,000, a simple $10 donation (the minimum required) could help save ten lives. And, with that, "10 for 10" became their slogan, and they ended up winning their very first daily prize of $1,000!

With their confidence flying high, Amy and her volunteers began to devote every waking hour of every day to the challenge, and quickly recruited college students to help out, keenly aware that their reach on Facebook would be much greater. Sororities at Ohio State and Rutgers University pounded the pavement, going door-to-door in dormitories to raise money. Even high school students were contacting their friends, who were voting and donating at least $10.

Amy and her brigade also sent e-mails to their list of 8,000 supporters with detailed instructions on how to donate. They blogged about the Charity Challenge and asked others to blog as well. Yahoo! Groups focused toward adoptive parents helped spread the word. And nurses took their computers to the hospital to reach out to their extensive network of colleagues for support.

Everyone worked frenetically to get the job done, and with each passing day, Love Without Boundaries was winning more and more mini-challenges—ultimately walking away with thirteen of them, totaling $13,000 in prize money.

But, still, hearts were set on the $50,000—both literally and figuratively. And as the challenge neared completion, Love Without Boundaries was neck and neck with Free Tibet—a student-run group whose goal was to raise money so they could fly to Beijing and protest against China. The irony was profound, given that Love Without Boundaries was a humanitarian organization dedicated to supporting China in its own way.

Both groups, in a heated fight to the finish, pulled out all the stops. Only one organization, they knew, would be victorious in the end.

The challenge was finally over in early February 2008, and all they could do was wait out the thirty-day period that

Facebook needed to tally the votes fairly. In mid-March, Amy received the call she'd been so anxiously awaiting.

Love Without Boundaries had won the $50,000! And between that, the $13,000 in combined daily winnings, and the money raised in donations, the organization took home a whopping $125,000.

As promised in their "10 to 10" mantra, the $50,000 saved over ten children with heart defects, and the remainder of the money was divided between their five other programs, including Healing Homes, which offers otherwise destitute babies safe and warm environments to thrive in by providing trained nannies to feed the children and surgeries to correct their cleft lips at the first possible opportunity.

While winning the Facebook Charity Challenge certainly had a direct fiscal impact, the victory also set in motion a viral effect, promising both immediate and long-term success for the organization. Not only had they attracted a wide range of new donors, but they'd also more than doubled their e-mail list.

Today, with nearly 150 volunteers in thirty-eight states and nine countries worldwide—but still no office and no noteworthy overhead costs—Love Without Boundaries is supporting more than 1,500 children in 100 orphanages across China, on an annual operating budget of $1.6 million. They're running five schools (and looking at opening up their sixth imminently), and have close to 300 children in their foster care programs in fourteen different orphanages, for whom they provide everything from cribs to warm clothing. Many of these children are now being adopted both domestically and abroad.

Love Without Boundaries has assigned one volunteer to be their official Facebook coordinator, responsible for dedicating one hour each day to updating their Facebook page with any new and important stories or information.

"Facebook changed the whole way that our foundation operates," says Amy, reflecting on their remarkable progress—the most recent of which was winning another $35,000 contest unrelated to the social networking site. "We are now using social media in a much bigger way; we understand its importance. The Facebook challenge really showed us what we needed to do. Not to mention that it brought us over thirteen thousand new members, and we also now receive regular donations through Facebook."

Aside from the sixty to seventy hours a week Amy devotes to Love Without Boundaries—which only holds one face-to-face meeting a year—how does she think it's possible that such a small charity could slay the many philanthropic giants in its way?

"We do anything we can to raise money for the kids. People support us and vote for us because they believe in what we're doing. In today's economy, people want to know their hard-earned donations are honestly making a difference. We're changing the lives of kids each day. It's really that simple."

SIXTEEN

LAWYER *Speak*

When Rebecca Phillips graduated from Bob Jones University in May of 2005 and entered Notre Dame Law School the following fall, life was simple—as simple as it could be, that is, for a first-year law student.

FACEBOOK *Fairytales*

Having spent four years at Bob Jones—a conservative Christian college and seminary in Greenville, South Carolina—Rebecca relished her new and notably less stringent environment. She no longer needed to wear dresses and panty hose to class each day. Nor was she banned from men's dormitories after curfew or discouraged from holding hands in public with members of the opposite sex.

While these allowances may have been commonplace for most, for Rebecca and the two other Bob Jones alums at Notre Dame, they represented a mutual bond—a nod to their shared experiences in BJU's intense but academically fertile milieu. After all, Rebecca had enjoyed her undergrad years, despite the conventional framework.

Still, she was eager to expose herself to new opportunities, so, during her second semester at Notre Dame, Rebecca decided to join Facebook, the virtually ubiquitous social networking site that had been prohibited at BJU.

Rebecca explored the site's many features and noticed that there were a variety of different groups that had been formed by students just like her. *Why not start one for Bob Jones alums?* Rebecca thought, setting her plan in motion.

There was only one glitch. At the time, Facebook groups were limited to those with the same domain name—in other words, Rebecca's Bob Jones group would only be available to those students who'd graduated from BJU, and, like her, had gone on to pursue their education at Notre Dame. But this didn't dissuade Rebecca, who enthusiastically set up "Bob Jones University Survivors"—a tongue-in-cheek nod to her alma mater's infamously austere reputation. She didn't anticipate that the group would attract more than five members, but it didn't matter; it was all in good fun, and a way to keep up with her fellow alums.

Not long after, though, Facebook opened up group membership across educational networks, and "Bob Jones University Survivors" developed into a family of twelve, half of whom Rebecca had never met.

In a matter of months, with a lively series of discussions under way—topics ranged from religion and theology to school policies and current events—the group ballooned to 400, then 600, and, ultimately, to over 1,000 members, purely by word of mouth. There were ex–faculty members, graduates from the '60s and '70s, and a large contingent of former BJU debate teamers, which included Rebecca.

In the fall of 2006, during her sophomore year at Notre Dame, one of Rebecca's fellow debate team alums—who wasn't a member of the group, but had observed its discussion board with interest—reached out via Facebook. He wrote:

Hi Rebecca,

I'm a lawyer in the Chicago area. I can definitely appreciate the plight of Bob Jones students and graduates, since I've been through it. I wanted to get in touch with you because I think your discussion group is very interesting, and it's great to see where fellow Bob Jones debate team members have ended up. Notre Dame is a fantastic law school.

I might have some contacts in the area if you're interested. I don't know what field of law you're pursuing, but if there's anything that I can do to help you—even if it's just to give you advice on how to handle the Bob Jones name on your résumé—let me know.

Regards,

John

Flattered by the gesture, Rebecca replied, saying that she would certainly take him up on his offer if the occasion arose, and the two became Facebook friends, corresponding back and forth for a short time. She was pleased that the liveliness of her group had drawn such positive attention, but had no idea that this attention was about to explode.

On February 28, 2007, one of Rebecca's friends, and a member of "Bob Jones University Survivors," initiated a controversial thread on the group's page, which read:

I just ran across the following paragraph in a history book that made me sick:

"When Governor George Wallace stood in the doorway of the University of Alabama to prevent a black student from registering, Bob

Jr. awarded him an honorary doctorate and praised him as 'David, warring against the giant, Tyranny.' "

There are many, many examples of clear racism in our alma mater's past. Have you ever had someone pull back in surprise when they found out you went to BJU because of the racism that was institutionalized and publicly expressed for so long? How do we cope with that as grads? What can the school do to expunge their guilt and move on?

A nearly year-long heated dialogue ensued: *It's damaging our reputation! We want to be proud of our school, not ashamed! We need to do something about it!*

Members fervently voiced their opinions, until one young man had a revolutionary idea, and sent Rebecca the following note:

Would you mind if we spin your group off into another group, which we can use to fine-tune an open letter to BJU asking them to do something about this overt racism?

Rebecca was intrigued, and without hesitation urged him to draft a letter and post it on both the wall of the new group—called "Please Reconcile"—and on an independent website, where their comrades in arms could make their own suggestions and changes.

Winter turned to spring, and as the extensive editing proceeded, Rebecca pursued her final semester in law school, frantically searching for a full-time job.

One day another message from John appeared in her Facebook in-box:

How's your job search going? Is there anything I can do to help?

Rebecca could hardly believe her luck, replying:

I'm not opposed to moving to the Chicago area. If you have contacts at any law firms, I'd be most grateful!

John responded:

Actually, my firm might be hiring an associate. It's a small, very specialized firm, and I'm not sure what you're looking to do. But if you're interested, let me know.

Hastily, Rebecca researched his firm, which—to her delight—handled mostly civil rights law, one of her foremost passions. She followed up by sending her résumé, and come the end of March, had interviewed with all three partners.

By the last week of school, Rebecca was gainfully employed, ready to head to the Windy City to embark on her new life and career.

But when she landed at her new firm, John had some surprising information to share. Not only had he been intrigued by her "Bob Jones University Survivors" group, but he was also still connected to the university—the university to which Rebecca and her cohorts were about to send their letter on racial relations.

Panicked, she approached her boss, who handled the situation with dignity, assuring her, "This will not impact your position at the firm and will not affect our professional relationship." A fortunate circumstance for Rebecca, because a few months later, in November 2008, the "Please Reconcile" group—consisting of 500 members, at least 450 of them BJU alumni—sent their open letter to every member of the school's board, asking them to make a statement of "regret and reconciliation" about the school's past policies on race. It read:

Dear Dr. Stephen Jones, Bob Jones University Board of Trustees, and Administration:

We are Bob Jones University alumni and students who care deeply about our alma mater. We recognize that God has used the university in our lives for good, and we pray that God preserves the university and uses it in the lives of those who come after us. We value our time there, the many wonderful faculty and staff members who taught us and touched our lives, the godly friends we met, and the school's fearless stand for Jesus Christ.

We are troubled, though, by certain aspects of the school's reputation regarding its attitude toward the topic of racial discrimination. The school is widely known as segregationist, bigoted, and racist. Some of us were not aware of this reputation while we attended the university and were baffled when we encountered negative perceptions from others after we graduated. Our ignorance may be to the university's credit, since it suggests that the actual practices of the university have improved beyond the older perceptions that persist in the world at large.

Nevertheless, the reputation remains. We see it in people's faces and hear it in their comments and reactions upon learning where we went to school. Sometimes we encounter it in job interviews—troubling times to be confronted about racial prejudice. For some of us, employees suspect our motives as employers. Those of us who are ministers and spiritual leaders must explain our association with the university to minority congregants. All of us are charged to present the Gospel, but must now do so in the context of this stigma. After a period of objective discussion and research, we begin to understand the origin of these negative impressions.

LAWYER *Speak*

The university's historical position on the topic of racial discrimination is deeply troubling, including stories of its founding leaders having connections to notoriously bigoted characters and organizations. Some of that history is disturbingly recent. Married black students were not admitted until 1971, and unmarried black students were not admitted until 1975. Even then, a ban on interracial relationships lasted into the twenty-first century. Records from those years include vicious and embarrassing statements from people representing the university in an official capacity. The individuals on the receiving end of this treatment recounted those experiences to their tight-knit communities, and their stories provided a public record of the university's attitude toward minorities. Finally, many of us have personally seen actions or heard statements from current members of the university community which seem to indicate that sensitivity toward this issue is not a priority of its administration or representatives.

We realize that other institutions have made mistakes as well. We do not excuse their mistakes, but neither are we concerned with them. They are responsible for what they have done, and many of them have issued public statements of regret and apology and have taken dramatic steps to demonstrate their commitment to change. Bob Jones University, to our knowledge, has never done so. We can find no record of a statement that admits that the university's historical position on the topic of racial discrimination, while sincere, was mistaken, and God has granted a better perspective. We are writing to request that such a statement be made, backed up by concrete actions that demonstrate its seriousness.

We hope and believe that such a statement would be sincere and accurate. We recognize that it may be difficult to make and realize that it may attract criticism from other corners. That is why we want you to know that should such a statement be made, we will support it completely and joyfully.

God's glory is the absolute supreme goal; and this behavior and unyielding "standing without apology" is not only unbecoming but completely undermining of that Gospel of grace to which the university so vehemently claims to adhere.

We request this not just to remove stumbling blocks in our dealings with others, or to improve appraisals of our résumés (though we believe it will do both); we hope that you will choose to address this issue because of your own conviction that all people, regardless of their skin color or ethnicity, are made in the image of God and that God desires unity in His Church.

We pray that you will do this, most of all, because it will be doing right and showing forth a true demonstration of the love and humility that God desires from His people.

The letter was also posted on both of Rebecca's Facebook groups. And while the board never responded directly, Bob Jones did issue a statement on their website, apologizing for the school's "failures" in race relations policies during its eighty-one-year history:

Like any human institution, we have failures as well. For almost two centuries American Christianity, including BJU in its early stages, was characterized by the segregationist ethos of American culture. Consequently, for far too long, we allowed institutional policies regarding race to be shaped more directly by that ethos than by the principles and precepts of the Scriptures. We conformed to the culture rather than provide a clear Christian counterpoint to it. In so doing, we failed to accurately represent the Lord and to fulfill the commandment to love others as ourselves. For these failures we are profoundly sorry.

Rebecca was elated! "It's completely amazing. Not only did this Facebook group, which started with only three members, help me get a job, but it was the catalyst for a historic turn of events at one of the country's most distinguished universities," she reflects. "Writing that open letter was such a distinctly collaborative effort. But I guess that's the magic of Facebook—it brings together people who are passionate about the same thing, and, in this case, it was a providentially perfect mix of skill sets."

Rebecca adds, "At first, most of the people in the 'Bob Jones Survivors' group were just names and avatars to me, but through all of this we've become friends. We're hoping to get together for a barbecue back in Greenville next year."

SEVENTEEN

FUELING THE *Fire*

*A*vi Savar had spent over fifteen years as a television producer—from music and sports to pop culture, he'd done it all. His résumé, in fact, read a bit like a channel guide.

He'd launched his media career at USA Network, transitioned to short-form live programming at Showtime, then landed the coveted position of entertainment producer for ABC's breakfast gabfest, *Good Morning America*, and, ultimately, had decided to broaden his repertoire by moving to Viacom, where he produced VH1's *The Fabulous Life*—a fast-paced series affording viewers behind-the-scenes access to the lives of the rich and famous.

But despite the benefits of his glamorous day job—a steady paycheck and an executive position within a dominant corporate conglomerate—Avi desired something more. He needed to spread his proverbial wings.

And in the spring of 2004, that's just what he did, with the inauguration of Big Fuel—his own entertainment company, devoted to creating content, graphics, and animation for long-form programming. Shortly thereafter, VH1—his former employer—became a client, and Avi forged ahead with his plan: to entice other big-name businesses to join his swiftly evolving roster. After all, most start-ups were destined for failure, and, like every other entrepreneur with a concept and a dream, Avi wasn't prepared to become a statistic.

For the next six months he worked tirelessly, honing his brand and developing his enterprise, until the unthinkable happened. Big Fuel signed a deal with uber-media-giant America Online, instantly catapulting them from greenness to seeing green—in their pocket.

Aside from the blatant financial boost, though, Big Fuel saw another transformation. With AOL on board, the company began producing high-volume, short-form Web programming, rather than their standard made-for-TV content. It was something they'd never done before, but, surprisingly, the shift made a great deal of sense in the context of Avi's professional history.

At *GMA*, he'd generated three- to five-minute segments which had consisted of a beginning, middle, and end, which—as it turned out—translated seamlessly to short-form Web programming. He was even able to easily adapt his VH1 experience with hour-long pop culture shows, which had been broken down into individual segments.

By May of 2005, within a year of starting the company, Big Fuel had churned out 150 "webisodes"—brief episodes that aired on the Internet as opposed to on broadcast or cable television—before anyone even knew what they were.

Avi was on top of the world, as his ever-expanding venture swelled to success. Before long, the company was also manufacturing both music and Latino programming for AOL. And with four different franchises to speak of, Big Fuel launched *Acceso Total*, a series of single-subject, celebrity pop culture shows for the vast global Internet service.

All of a sudden, Avi's business model had gotten a major facelift. He'd gone from producing five television episodes over X number of months to producing 500 webisodes over the same period of time. It was fast-paced, for sure, but he relished the radical progression, as brands and agencies began knocking down his door, eager for a piece of the action. *How was Big Fuel getting their message and the messages of their clients across to consumers in this revolutionary fashion?* At once, it seemed, the former entertainment television producer had become a veritable guru in the world of syndicating online video—through social networks, publishers, and blogs. He knew what worked, what didn't, and, most importantly, how to transmute brands into innovative programming and content.

Things were on track at Big Fuel—so much so that Avi wasn't seeking any immediate renovations. *Why mess with a good thing?*

But, by the fall of 2006, one just happened to fall into his lap. A new social networking site called Facebook—previously reserved for educational institutions—had been extended to anyone with a registered e-mail address. Avi, who was already a member of every social network known to man—even if he didn't use them regularly—joined immediately.

At first, he wasn't quite sure how Facebook could benefit Big Fuel, or what level of impact it could have on the achievements of his company. He'd done his research and knew that, historically, every time a new channel of communication emerged, there were opportunities and expertise developed around those channels. *But what was different about Facebook? And would it be able to stand out in the already-crowded pool of social media networks?*

Avi was determined to figure out how to navigate the new channel and, above all, how to inspire people to use it as a means of sharing their message. This determination quickly turned into reasoning.

Facebook, he deduced, wouldn't be an effective medium for delivering overt product messaging because the human component was too prevalent. Yet it was still a tool that enabled delivery of communications—whether it was a personal status update, a link to a news article, or a video. What he had to do, he realized, was find a way to integrate product placement into these communications without explicitly promoting said products—something only a television producer–cum–Web content whiz would be capable of.

Then it dawned on him: The uniqueness of Big Fuel was that they were still, in part, an entertainment company—an entertainment company that told people's stories. And Avi knew that the most important aspect of producing is to understand your target audience. If, for example, he was to create a travel show for VH1, it would be drastically different than the same premise on, say, The Travel Channel. It would look completely different. It would sound completely different. It would, overall, have a completely different feel.

With this in mind, Avi and his team set out to bridge the gap between entertainment and social media by appealing to Facebook members via targeted content in the form of story-centric videos and games that people would be inspired to pass along to their friends.

Essentially, Big Fuel began reaching out to Facebookers in the same way a public relations firm would approach an editor or writer. When Avi had a new piece of content that his group wanted to spread across the social landscape, he'd start by contacting his vast network of 700+ friends, saying, "Hey, check this out. It's our latest, greatest game. Play it, and if you like it, share it," which—invariably—they did.

On occasion, Big Fuel even offered incentives or rewards contingent on furthering the domino effect. But, no matter what, they always remained true to their "golden rule": *Keep everything social, so people don't feel like we're shoving advertorials down their throats*—a recipe for success in their perpetual pursuit of credibility.

But it wasn't always as easy as it sounds. Avi and his team were forced to think outside the box—to continually craft new ways of embedding their clients' products within a storytelling framework.

In order for an ad campaign to work on the Facebook platform, they decided, it had to pass their "6 A.M. test," which centered on the following premise:

When people wake up in the morning, they're not thinking about how to purchase the cheapest toilet paper or which sponge will wipe out the most grease. They're thinking about getting their kids off to school as quickly as possible, which train to catch to work, or how to pay their mounting bills. In short, they're thinking about personal issues, which may or may not be enhanced by products they don't know they need.

The conclusion: *If, at 6 A.M., an ad wouldn't grab people's attention, then it wasn't worth Big Fuel's efforts.*

With each new account, Avi asked himself the same question: *Will this pass the 6 A.M. test?*

"We either have to entertain people or help them," he could often be heard explaining to his crew—a mantra that paid off. Soon, more and more companies were approaching Avi for a video, game, or Facebook application, saying, "We want you to help us reach this particular demographic."

For a major consumer packaged-goods brand, Big Fuel worked with College Humor to create a two-and-a-half-minute "Real-Life Twitter" video geared toward college students with just one quick mention of their product. Another high-profile client benefited from product integration through five episodes of "How to Remodel Your Bathroom"—content that was not only informative, but *useful* to its audience.

Perhaps one of Big Fuel's most inventive promotions was an eight-episode reality series, titled *One Less Stress*, highlighting Neutrogena's new acne-stress-control cream—designed for sixteen- to twenty-one-year-old girls—through strategically honed segments covering a wide range of age-appropriate themes—from relationship issues and parental problems to financial woes. They flew in "real" young women from various regions of the United States, and even recruited *Seventeen* magazine's fashion editor to appear in a segment on style.

There were Neutrogena graphics, sure, but not once was the pimple ointment patently pushed. Big Fuel then took each individual episode and distributed it through Facebook, which gave rise to triumphant results—just one example of their indispensability to partners such as AOL, FOX, and NBC, in addition to the brands and clients they were trying to promote.

Social media, namely Facebook, had become a fundamental component of Big Fuel's fabric and how they thought about the world of content marketing. They even created a video called "Facebook Manners," which garnered a larger audience than an episode of Avi's previously helmed TV show, *The Fabulous Life*. The difference was, promoting via Facebook didn't cost a thing.

Over the course of five years, Avi had watched his brainchild undergo a sweeping transformation, with their social media efforts skyrocketing from 0 percent at inception to upwards of 80 percent a half-decade later.

"We're a completely different company because of Facebook. Now, we're all about leveraging new media and new channels of communications. Social media, inherently, is a unique way of delivering messages. There's no corporate behavior involved. It's about individuals, and

I think that's very misunderstood by the general public. Brands are providing real value to real people, and I'm grateful for that. I'm certain that Facebook will continue to evolve, and—with Facebook—Big Fuel will evolve as well," Avi speculates.

Laughing, he then adds, "I think it was the day my mom joined Facebook and started posting on my wall when I realized just how mainstream the site really is!"

EIGHTEEN

FULL *Circles*

*W*hen Jodi Singer was twelve years old, her grandmother presented her with a very special gift—a gold and diamond initial ring in the shape of a "J."

"I want you to own something of value," her grandmother told her. "I've had it for some time, but I waited until you were old enough, so you could find a place to hide it."

Jodi understood. Having endured a dreadful childhood with a mother who was prone to stealing and verbal abuse, she'd never bothered to seek out worldly possessions. Why would she? Her mother would surely have pilfered them and sold them off for cash.

But, despite her grandmother's logical request, Jodi couldn't resist. The next day, admiring her new possession glistening in the palm of her hand, she slipped it onto her finger. The ring made her feel special—an uncommon feeling for Jodi, given her mother's relentless mistreatment. And, for the next four years, she rarely took it off—except, of course, when she was with her grandmother.

At sixteen years of age, following her sophomore year in high school, Jodi's father—who hadn't been married to her mother for some time—offered to send her off to England for a summer exchange program. She was beyond thrilled at the opportunity to experience European culture and visit sites like Big Ben and Buckingham Palace. Above all, though, Jodi was just happy to get out of her house and away from her mother.

Two months later, returning home from her trip, ready to regale her friends and family with every salacious detail about her very first jaunt overseas, Jodi arrived at her mother's house to find all of her belongings on the front porch.

"I'm sorry, but you've got to go," her mother said matter-of-factly. "I've already made arrangements for you to live with your father."

Jodi's heart sank. It wasn't that she didn't want to live with her father, his new wife, and their new baby in their tiny apartment in New Jersey. But why did it always have to be such a drama? Couldn't her mother have given her the chance to pack her own things—to say good-bye to her room and to the house where she'd grown up, even if the memories weren't pleasant ones?

Jodi knew she had no choice, so she went to live with her father, whom she adored unconditionally—and the feelings were mutual. Things were tight financially, but Jodi didn't care. She was mostly happy to be out of her formerly abusive environment, and, after all, she didn't want for much.

Until, of course, it came time to buy her senior class ring. With a hefty $500 price tag, she was pretty sure her father wouldn't be able to afford it. But she simply *had* to have one. All the other kids were getting them, and they were just *so* awesome; she truly felt her life would be incomplete without one.

"Dad, I have to ask you something," Jodi said, approaching him after school one afternoon. "It's time to buy my senior class ring. Can you help me out?"

"Aren't you a junior?" He smiled, putting his arm around his daughter affectionately.

"Yes, but you order your senior ring a year ahead. I really, really, really want one. Please?"

"How much are they?"

"Five hundred dollars." Jodi scrunched her face to indicate that she understood the soaring cost.

"I wish I could, sweetie, but I can't afford something like that right now. I'm really sorry."

Distraught, Jodi walked away with her head down, determined to find a way to get her ring. And for the subsequent days, she proceeded to beg her father at every available opportunity to *please* buy a class ring for her.

Eventually, he gave in, and Jodi was not only overjoyed but touched. She knew what a financial sacrifice it had been for him, realizing that he'd likely had to sell something of value to scrounge together the money.

"I bought you the ring because I know how important it is to you," he told her. "And because I know you love soccer, and I love watching your games."

Jodi could barely wait until it arrived—she'd selected a vibrant turquoise blue stone and, naturally, there'd be a soccer ball to represent her favorite school sport. She'd never take the ring off, she vowed.

But four months later, after her prized possession had arrived, the unexpected occurred.

Out one night with friends at The Underground nightclub in New York City, Jodi came home to find her ring finger bare. As if that wasn't bad enough, her "J" ring had vanished as well. The next evening, she searched her girlfriend's house, where she'd gotten ready prior to going out. It had to be there. But it wasn't. They then tore apart her friend's car. Again, nothing. Jodi knew she couldn't exactly call the club, since she was way too young to have been there in the first place, and had used a fake ID to gain entrance. She was devastated. And she didn't have the heart to tell her father—especially after all he'd gone through to purchase the ring for her.

Fourteen years passed with Jodi holding on to her secret. Married to her second husband—with a ten-year-old son—she called her father to impart some bad news. She'd had a miscarriage, she told him. She was deeply sad, she said, but she'd be okay. He told her he loved her, as always, and at 6 P.M. they said good night.

The following morning at seven o'clock, the phone rang, startling Jodi out of a sound sleep. Her husband came into the bedroom and knelt down by her side.

"Father died," he said.

Jodi awoke immediately. Her husband's father had long suffered from a heart condition and had just been released from the hospital, but they certainly hadn't expected him to pass away so soon.

"I'm so sorry," she said, holding her husband in her arms. "My heart is breaking for you."

"No, Jodi. It's your father," he said sorrowfully.

"That's impossible!" she cried. "I just spoke to him." Her eyes flooded with tears, and soon, she was sobbing. "He was active, he was healthy; he'd just turned fifty. He didn't have a gray hair on his head! How did this happen?!"

"Your stepmother said he fell out of bed and hit his head."

The details were fuzzy, but Jodi paid little attention. All she could focus on was that her precious father, her best friend in the entire world, was gone—just like that. First the miscarriage, then her dad; it was too much for any one person to handle.

Jodi spent the next ten years mourning her loss each and every day, wishing she had her class ring to remember her father by.

In December of 2008—exactly a decade to the month from Jodi's father's passing—she received a message from a stranger via Facebook. Jodi had only joined the social networking site three weeks prior, at the suggestion of an old high school friend who'd convinced her to sign up in order to locate two of their other childhood best friends. The note read:

Hi Jodi,

You don't know me, but I have two rings that I think might belong to you. Can you please give me some information about yourself and the rings so I can confirm they're yours?

Regards,

Denise Mazza Hand

Jodi's first reaction was skepticism. She was, frankly, unaccustomed to good things happening to her out of the blue. It hadn't exactly been her life's pattern. But

Jodi wrote back, regardless, intrigued by the woman's claim.

Denise, it turned out, had recently visited her mother's apartment in Manhattan and had come across an old jewelry box in Denise's childhood bedroom. Denise had taken it home with her, expecting to sell off some of the pricier items—tokens from old boyfriends and such—when she found the rings she'd picked up twenty-two years earlier in the bathroom at The Underground nightclub.

The women exchanged messages—Denise having only just become a member of Facebook as well—and Jodi was able to identify both her class ring (by the soccer ball and turquoise stone) and the "J" ring her grandmother had given her all those years ago.

"I knew they were yours, because the class ring had your name inscribed inside," Denise told her. "I tried to locate you for years after I found them, but Jodi Singer isn't exactly an uncommon name!"

"I don't know how I can ever thank you for this," Jodi said. "You have no idea how much these rings mean to me."

One week later, Jodi's rings arrived on her doorstep, and she could barely believe her good fortune, calling everyone she knew to relay the amazing story.

"How can I repay Denise?" she asked each person she spoke to. "Flowers don't seem to cover it."

Determined to pay it forward, Jodi wrote letters to the local newspapers and international television stations—CNN, ABC, FOX—detailing the story and asking them to give Denise the recognition she deserved. And even though Jodi never heard back, she felt that, at the very least, she'd made her father proud.

Eight weeks passed, and in February 2009, Jodi's luck took a turn for the worse again. She was diagnosed with colon cancer and would have a long road to recovery ahead of her. Jodi, single again with two sons—eighteen and eight years old—decided to move from New Jersey to Florida, where her aunt, her only devoted family member, could take care of her and help support her in the fight of her life.

As she made the long drive south—to Lantana, near Delray Beach, where she'd spent every summer with her paternal grandparents—Jodi couldn't help but feel her father's presence around her.

"So many horrible things have happened to me, between my childhood, two failed marriages, and now my cancer," Jodi acknowledges. "All of a sudden, this person came out of nowhere and did such a fantastic thing by returning my rings. It reminded me that the world isn't horrible. I wouldn't call myself a spiritual person, but I do believe things happen for a reason. And I have faith that my father—in some unidentifiable way—made sure I got those rings. I don't know how or why. I guess maybe he just knew I'd need them now more than ever."

NINETEEN

UNDER *Attack*

*I*t was springtime in New York. The smell of hot dogs and salty pretzels permeated the streets as locals flocked to Central Park, eager to soak in the fresh, warm air—a precursor to the balmy summer ahead.

FACEBOOK *Fairytales*

Ariel Schwartz, a recent graduate of Barnard College at Columbia University and the Jewish Theological Seminary of America (both on the Upper West Side of the city) was preparing for the adventure of her life. In two months, she'd depart for Mumbai, India, to work as a volunteer for the American Jewish Joint Distribution Committee, the overseas arm of the American Jewish community, focused on rescuing Jews at risk, relieving Jews in need, and renewing Jewish community life abroad.

Aware that the Indian-Jewish population had been prevalent in Mumbai for over two thousand years, Ariel was eager to help further their education and leadership initiatives, and to support their overall sense of worth as a community.

Arriving in early July of 2008, Ariel was enthusiastic and anxious at the same time. She planned to spend a full year, living thousands of miles away from family and friends, in a country with a history of terrorist activity.

But, before long, four months had passed, and Ariel had easily adapted to life in Mumbai. She'd made a number of friends through her own organization and other similar groups, and had found Chabad House, a source of Jewish life and practice, primarily utilized by Jewish travelers or visitors, and an epicenter of Judaism in the city. The Jewish outreach center had quickly become a home away from home for Ariel, who'd fostered particularly close relationships with their rabbi and his wife.

212

UNDER *Attack*

For perhaps the first time since finishing school, Ariel felt relaxed and content in her new and drastically different environment. That is, until Wednesday, November 26, the day before Thanksgiving.

Ariel, along with her boyfriend and her roommate, were gathered in the kitchen, baking apple crisp. They'd planned to host a sizable holiday get-together the following day, with all of their local Indian, Jewish, and American friends. There was a lot of cooking to be done, and as they laughed and prepped the food together, they had no idea what was taking place just twenty minutes away in downtown Mumbai.

The phone rang, cutting through the chorus of casual banter.

"Hello?" Ariel answered, expecting to hear from one of her forthcoming guests. Maybe they'd ask if they could contribute a bottle of wine or an extra side dish.

"Ariel, I'm so glad you're home!" her friend's panicked voice came across the line. "Don't go downtown. There are shootings. They think it's some kind of gang warfare."

Shocked, Ariel hung up the phone and alerted her companions to the terrifying news. She'd spent most of her time in Mumbai precisely where the shootings were taking place. The downtown area was like the Times Square of Mumbai, with shops, restaurants, and loads of tourists.

The phone rang again. It was another friend, with more bad news.

"Something is going on at Chabad House. Shootings. Gang warfare. Definitely stay away."

"Are the shootings related to religion?" she asked, fearful for her friends and herself.

"Nobody knows for sure."

Ariel was heartbroken. Chabad had been her support system, her familiar safe haven in an unfamiliar land. She'd been there just four days earlier for Shabbat services on Friday night, into Saturday.

During the ensuing hours, Ariel's phone rang off the hook with this warning or that from friends, neighbors, and coworkers.

With no television to switch on, Ariel immediately dialed into her Indian computer network, desperate for information on the hysteria only minutes away. Every news website reported the same thing. There was a riotous gang war in downtown Mumbai, and as the night progressed, it became clear that the gang war was actually a full-fledged terrorist attack.

In a state of suspended alarm, Ariel called her parents in New York to let them know that she was okay. She didn't know exactly what was going on, she said, but she was in her apartment, shielded from danger. She told them not to worry—a futile directive, she understood, given the current state of affairs.

Late into the night, Ariel and her roommate fielded calls from their supervisors at the American Jewish Joint Distribution Committee offices in New York, Israel, and India. Talking back and forth between their cell phones and the landline in either hand, they were told to stay put and await further instructions.

Ariel was eager to notify her extended family and friends that she was okay, but with over 1 billion people in India and 14 million in Mumbai, the phone lines quickly flooded, and, before long, her calling capabilities became spotty at best. Lines were crossed. Busy signals buzzed in her ear. And she felt helpless, a prisoner in her own apartment, with no way of connecting to most of her loved ones, who—by that point—were undoubtedly tuned in to the situation overseas.

She could get online, but certainly couldn't e-mail hundreds of people. That's when her next move became obvious. Facebook.

The social networking site had experienced rampant growth while Ariel had been in college, and was therefore a natural means of communication between her and hundreds of her friends. Even her mother, sister, aunts, uncles, and cousins were members. It would be the perfect means of keeping everyone up-to-date at the same time while she remained in lockdown. It would also be a welcome distraction from the ubiquitous anxiety.

As soon as she logged on to her page, Ariel was overwhelmed. Her wall had been inundated with pleas for information. Where was she? Was she okay? Did she know what was happening? Was she going to leave the country? *Could* she leave the country? Was it safe to go outside? Were the attacks targeting certain people/religions? Who were the terrorists?

And her in-box, too, was filled with hundreds of messages. Ariel posted a status update:

Thank you all so much for your concern. I'm okay. Everyone I know is okay. Right now, we're hiding out in our apartment. I'll keep everyone posted as often as possible.

For the next twenty-four hours, Ariel stayed in close touch with her organization and updated her Facebook status hourly, to the great relief of her extended network.

At six o'clock on Thursday, Thanksgiving evening, Ariel received a call from her organization's supervisor.

"Pack your bags. We're thinking about evacuating you. It might be to Austria. It might be home to America. Be ready."

Ariel couldn't help but flash back to 9/11 and acknowledge the parallel to 26/11 (the date of the current attacks, as formatted in India). There was no way of knowing if the terrorists were targeting the foreign Jewish community, and as she was part of that community, evacuating, while inherently frightening, did seem like the best option.

After all, she was hardly inconspicuous. In America, you could be in New York City, Chicago, or Philadelphia—any major city—and be of any background, religion, race, or ethnicity, and fit in. But abroad, that wasn't always the case. Mumbai, specifically, was very homogenous. If you weren't Indian, Bangladeshi, Pakistani, Sri Lankan, or Nepali, you stood out like a sore thumb.

Ariel had become all too aware of this fact on her daily walks to work, when she'd been ogled by passersby—or when she'd called the neighborhood restaurant from which they'd frequently order dinner. Inevitably, her American accent would give her away, allowing the person on the other end of the line to recognize her instantly.

As she sat waiting impatiently to receive her marching orders, Ariel wondered where they'd go. It would be nice to visit Austria, preferably under better circumstances, but—either way—she was ready to flee.

At 9 P.M. her phone rang again.

"You need to get to the airport now," her supervisor instructed. "You have a flight that's leaving at eleven."

Not knowing how long she'd be gone, or even if she'd ever return to her apartment in India, Ariel updated her Facebook status one last time before she and her roommate threw their prepacked bags in the car and sped to the airport, where they were issued emergency evacuation tickets:

 I've been evacuated from my apartment, and I'm heading to the airport, ready to leave India. Everyone's well wishes have been a true source of support during this hectic and scary time. I'll let you all know where I am once I've arrived safely. For now, we've been advised

not to disclose our destination. Don't worry;
I'll be back on Facebook soon, and often.

Ariel was well aware that her cell phone wouldn't work in Israel—her secret destination—as it wasn't international, and only operable in India. Facebook, she suspected, would soon become her sole method of communication.

She was right. For the following two weeks, based in Jerusalem, Ariel took to Facebook to update friends, family, and even friends of friends and family as to her whereabouts and overall status. And when it was finally safe to return to India, Ariel made her many followers aware of her plans.

While the Indian-Jewish community remained shaken, Ariel couldn't let her nerves prevent her from finishing what she'd traveled so far to accomplish. In July 2009, Ariel completed her year in Mumbai—a year filled with both joy and peril.

"I was very fortunate not to have been among the many people killed in the terrorist attacks—and that I was able to keep my loved ones constantly up-to-date during an extremely trying and terrifying time," Ariel reflects. "I was so thankful to have Facebook, this amazing social network that people check persistently, especially in an emergency situation. When one person is living abroad in a country under attack, even if they're not your best friend, you get in touch with them. I had friends from elementary school, high school, and college tracking my every move."

Ariel adds, "While living in Mumbai may feel like eons ago, it was absolutely the most intense experience of my life."

TWENTY

DAMAGE *Control*

$\mathscr{B}$orn and raised in the Los Angeles area, Johnny Dam had one goal: to follow in the footsteps of every other Californian with a talent and a dream and become an entertainer—specifically, a comedian.

And in 1991, at thirty years old, he did just that. For twelve years, he traveled the country, warming up crowds, spouting one-liners, poking fun at clichéd relationship foibles, and mocking himself in the process. It was standard protocol for stand-up comics, and, while Johnny toiled to make ends meet by satirizing stereotypes, an unpleasant realization surfaced—he, too, had become a stereotype, an unsettling fact, to say the least.

But what could he really do about it? He'd devoted over a decade to the trial and error of developing and honing an act and a voice. He'd traversed thousands of miles on the road, competing with hundreds of other average, middle-aged, white-male comics with no real agenda outside of fueling a cheap laugh.

Sure, there'd been a time when effortless humor in exchange for twenty minutes of fame had seemed like enough, but—at forty-two years old, with a wife at home whom he rarely saw—Johnny knew he no longer wanted that for himself or for his family. He needed to define himself. He needed a purpose.

In 2005, determined to color outside the lines of his banal existence, Johnny took off for the Middle East, touring Iraq and Afghanistan to perform for the troops overseas. It was unlike anything he'd ever done before, and as a result of his eye-opening journey, it occurred to him that there might be a way to combine his gift for comedy and his understanding of social and political issues, and, in so doing, facilitate a new career.

Not long after his return, Johnny launched a show called *The DAMage Report* on the Internet television network, stream.tv, with the intention of building a one-stop comedy and news platform. His format, he decided, would be to select one topic for his weekly broadcast—something publicly relevant that he could still lampoon.

As weeks and months passed, Johnny struggled to establish a fan base, even turning to MySpace for ideas and publicity. He knew that the power of social networking was profound, but MySpace had limited capabilities, and he couldn't quite figure out how to apply it to his advantage.

Before long, he was adrift again, lost in the sea of Internet media, with a list of groupies he could count on one hand. He yearned to find focus and structure, a way to shape his show into an engaging and promotable package—something that his listeners could relate to and would revisit time and time again.

He was at a loss. In 2006, eager for inspiration, Johnny returned to the Middle East to entertain the troops once more. Even this, though, couldn't free him from his funk, and for the next two years he worked diligently, striving to make a name for himself outside the world of roving comics.

In February 2008, Johnny finally got a bit of a break when LA Talk Radio—an Internet radio station with no FCC oversight or officious corporate structure—picked up his show, *The DAMage Report*. Not only would he be given two hours, five days a week on the airwaves, but he'd also have the freedom to talk about whatever he wanted on the new call-in show. Even more promising was the fact that LA Talk Radio's vision—to be "irreverent, entertaining, and cool"—was perfectly aligned with Johnny's; instantly, things started to look up.

Each day, Johnny surfed any number of websites, the likes of Yahoo! and CNN, and read stacks of newspapers and magazines in an effort to gather material. His show still lacked structure, however—so much so that, typically, he had no idea what he was going to talk about even on his way to the station. Roughly eight months into his new gig, Johnny's amorphous approach really began to plague him. He needed to escape his rut. The dilemma was, he had no idea how.

Then came October of 2008. That's when Johnny decided to join Facebook. Having abandoned MySpace years earlier, he set up a personal page and began communicating with friends and fellow comedians—growing his list of contacts to 300. At first, it was nothing more than an amusing and welcome distraction from his day job.

Rummaging around the social networking site one morning before his two o'clock show, Johnny discovered an interesting component: He could link news articles to his Facebook page. A metaphoric lightbulb flashed. He didn't have to scour websites for hours each day, in search of topics he couldn't even be sure would entice his listeners. Instead, he could find articles, simply click on "share," and post them with his own commentary to his

Facebook wall—in advance of the show. This would give his audience a chance to arm themselves with knowledge and perhaps form their own opinions, thereby fostering continuous fodder for debate.

With his innovative approach in hand, Johnny set out to lay the groundwork for what he hoped would be a winning formula for *The DAMage Report*. Fortunately, it was just prior to the 2008 presidential election, and there was more than enough to scrutinize in the media.

One week later, his numbers had escalated dramatically, as had his Facebook fan base. Practically overnight, Johnny was freed up from having to agonize over material.

Sitting in his office one afternoon, the station manager appeared at his door with a wide smile. "Listen, Johnny. I don't know what you've done over the last couple of weeks, but your numbers have gone through the roof, and your show quality has drastically improved," he said. "It's finally structured. Don't get me wrong; you were funny before, but now you're funny with a purpose!"

Johnny beamed with pride, and for the months that followed, he forged ahead, drawing more and more followers from his Facebook podium. His audience quickly grew to thousands as his Facebook fans spread the word, creating a viral effect, unrivaled by anything he'd experienced to date.

Each morning, he'd wake up between 4 and 6 A.M., log on to the Internet to peruse his favorite news sites, pick five topics for the day—political and social—and, at ten o'clock, post them to his Facebook page, with his own opinion front and center. From there, his thousands of fans would go back and forth for four hours, commenting and arguing points until he went on-air at two o'clock—for an hour and fifty minutes straight, no commercial breaks, five days a week.

For the first time in nearly twenty years, Johnny felt heard. People were paying attention to what he had to say. They wanted to agree. They wanted to disagree. Either way, they were listening, as he expounded on the news behind the news. After all, he insisted, it was often what the media *wasn't* saying that was the most intriguing of all.

In March 2009, Johnny received one of the highest honors in his medium. He was named among "The Frontier Fifty: A Selection of Outstanding Talk Media Webcasters" by *Talkers* magazine, in the esteemed company of such big-league names as Adam Carolla, Dr. Laura Schlessinger, Sean Hannity, and the infamous Rush Limbaugh.

With his new streamlined format, thanks to Facebook, Johnny's workload was not only lightened, but he was also able to attract a stable of comics and experts who would appear live with him on a regular basis. He even developed an arts segment, determined to delve further into the arena of social relevance, a tactic that would grow his fan base even more.

DAMAGE *Control*

In the short space of a year, Johnny had 4,000 Facebook fans and a nationwide audience of 10,000. LA Talk Radio's *DAMage Report* was steadily flourishing. He had impressive followings, not only in California, but in Atlanta, Chicago, Florida, and New York. Even the troops in Iraq were tuning in.

Johnny couldn't ask for much more. Maybe a move to Sirius at some point, but—generally speaking—he felt satisfied with his achievements, and, best of all, he was having a blast doing what he loved.

Then, one day, guest host Mary Kennedy approached him with an idea: "My husband is a producer and listens to the show regularly," she said. "He has relationships with a couple of networks, and he introduced *The DAMage Report* to them. If you're interested, they'd like to see a pilot for a possible TV show."

Johnny paused momentarily. He'd been accustomed to having doors slammed in his face for so long that it was almost inconceivable to have such a once-in-a-lifetime opportunity drop into his lap.

"Let's do it!" he announced.

And that he did. A few weeks later—with over 300 radio shows under his belt—Johnny shot his very first pilot for national television.

If the former stand-up comic has his way, it'll be an hour-long, weekly show, during which Johnny—seated around a table with an intimate cluster of fellow comedians, actors, and activists—will follow his famous "five-topic" format.

"I see it as a nighttime gig, probably after eleven, since our subjects will often be adult-oriented," he explains. "And it'll be on cable. You'll never see me on one of the watered-down networks, like NBC or ABC. I like to go where people are willing to take chances."

Just as Johnny did with Facebook.

"I can say, without a doubt, that Facebook made my career. The people that I've met, the connections that I've made—they've been invaluable. Not to mention what it's done for my self-esteem," he laughs. "Facebook enabled me to communicate with like-minded people, to create structure for my show, and to become the online personality that I am. I've been told I have a huge Internet footprint now. If it wasn't for Facebook, I'd still be drifting around aimlessly with no real direction or purpose. Instead, I'm going to be a TV star!"

TWENTY-ONE

A STROKE OF *Luck*

In February 2009, Karin Linner was in the best shape of her life. At thirty-four years old, she'd been tackling triathlons for five years and was gearing up for her greatest athletic challenge to date: the Ironman—a series of long-distance races, consisting of a 2.4-mile swim, 112 miles on a bike, and a full marathon—to take place in Lake Placid in July.

The gargantuan feat may have seemed insurmountable to most, but Karin was barely fazed. She'd grown up in Sweden as a competitive swimmer and had already conquered the infamous Escape from Alcatraz and New York City triathlons three times—along with numerous other races—since her move to the Big Apple in the summer of 1996. Not only that, but Karin had been victorious in the elite amateur group—reserved for those just shy of being pro—and had won her age group on several occasions.

Having taken the year off in 2008 to recuperate, undergo minor foot surgery, and pursue her side business as a licensed sports massage therapist, the Ironman was set to be Karin's comeback, and she couldn't have been more prepared for the mammoth undertaking ahead of her.

Each morning, before heading to her day job at the investment bank where she worked in human resources, Karin would either run, bike, or swim, often doubling up her training sessions when she got home at the end of the day. On weekends she could be found biking up to 100 miles and running a minimum of 7. All she could think about was how energized she felt every morning when she woke up, and how accomplished she felt every night before going to bed.

Keeping in line with her stringent exercise routine, Karin ate healthfully—fish, fruits, and vegetables—and never junk food or McDonald's. And each year when she visited her primary-care physician, she'd get the same reaction: "I've never seen anyone with such good blood work. Your cholesterol must be the best in the City!"

On Sunday morning, February 8, true to form, Karin was raring to go, ready to embark on a seventy-five-mile-long bike ride with one of her friends. Despite it being the dead of winter, the active duo hit the pavement at 8 A.M., and, once they'd reached the halfway point, decided to stop for some tea at a coffee shop in Nyack, frequented by fellow cyclists.

"I have a strange headache." Karin confided in her friend. "It's like a dull pain."

"Let's go back then," she replied. "And don't push it!" Karin's friend was all too familiar with her companion's typically ambitious posture.

"I won't. I promise," Karin replied, smiling mischievously.

Back at home, Karin took a shower, popped some Motrin, and lay down for a nap, determined to get rid of her headache and to take advantage of the peace and quiet in her Brooklyn apartment. Her roommate was out of town and wouldn't return until the next day, and as Karin rested her head on the pillow, she couldn't help but relish the rare serenity surrounding her.

An hour later, Karin awoke, her head still throbbing. *That's weird*, she thought. *I never get headaches, much less persistent ones.*

She called a friend in Florida to distract herself from the nagging ache. They chatted for quite some time, catching each other up on the latest gossip. Just as Karin was about to hang up, her fingers started twitching. Before she knew what was happening, her right hand began flailing and she couldn't control it.

"*Noooo!*" Karin screamed, as her face went numb, followed by her right hand, and next her right leg, causing her entire body to crash to the ground.

She tried to cry out again, but her speech had been inexplicably cut off.

"What's happening, Karin?" Her friend was panicked on the other end of the line. "Are you okay? Is someone there? Say something!"

But she couldn't.

Soon enough, Karin started seizing, and, amid her fear and debilitation, deduced that she was having a stroke. Lucid enough to know time was of the essence, Karin mutely chanted three words in her head: *Don't die. Focus. Don't die. Focus.*

Unable to communicate with her friend, Karin stabbed at the phone—911, 911; she pressed the buttons repeatedly, until she realized the line was still active. She hung up and dialed again, unsure as to whether her friend had understood her objective.

But when the 911 operator picked up, Karin could do nothing more than squeak desperate noises, rendering a hardhearted reaction: "Who is this? What do you need?" the voice snapped, and then threatened, "If you don't tell me where you are and what's wrong with you, I can't help you."

Karin was desperate. She knew this man was her lifeline, so she gathered every bit of mental strength she had to give the number and street name of her location. She didn't even have the capacity to tell him she was in Brooklyn.

"Okay, we're sending someone."

Karin released a sigh of relief. Maybe she wouldn't die after all.

But there was still one problem. Her three-story building was practically as secure as Fort Knox. There'd be no way for them to get in, especially since her one and only neighbor worked weekends.

Mustering all of her energy, Karin dragged her limp body across the floor and managed to reach for her keys, which were—fortunately—hanging exactly where they were supposed to be.

Okay, next step, she coached herself, processing each action one at a time. She opened the door and propelled herself down the flight of stairs, landing behind the front door to her building. Able to unlock the door, Karin panted heavily, lying helpless in sweatpants and pink, fluffy slippers—her hair still damp from her post-workout shower.

After what seemed like an eternity, the ambulance finally arrived. Instantly, the paramedics realized that Karin was experiencing a stroke and transported her to Long Island College Hospital, one of the premier stroke centers, despite having originated from another hospital in Brooklyn.

Once at the hospital, the neurologist administered medication to break up Karin's blood clot, one which had to be dispensed within a confined amount of time to ensure any chance of survival. A few hours later, Karin underwent an angiogram and a stent placement in her carotid artery.

"There was a carotid dissection in your carotid artery, where it enters the brain," the doctor informed her. "That means the inner wall of the artery broke apart because there was either a specific trauma or an inherent weakness in the artery. It happens spontaneously. Since you didn't experience a trauma, your case is probably the latter. A clot formed, broke loose, and ended up in Broca's area, the region of the brain responsible for your speech production. You've been diagnosed with what's called apraxia of speech."

Karin looked at the doctor in silent alarm.

"There was no way you could have known about this, and there was nothing you could have done to avoid it," the doctor offered compassionately. "We're going to do everything we can to help you recover. You'll need to start speech therapy immediately and continue it in the long term."

Alone and scared, Karin managed to conjure up her father's phone number in Sweden, and also asked the hospital staff to contact a few close friends, realizing that she'd need a local support system.

In a short space of time, her friends arrived, promising to stick by her side at every turn. Her father flew in from

Sweden within a couple of days. But Karin was still discouraged that she couldn't communicate. She tried to write, but her penmanship came out like that of a child. She'd see a word on the page, know it wasn't right, but—for the life of her—she couldn't figure out what was wrong with it.

"We know what you mean," her friends would encourage. "You don't need to get the spelling just right."

Karin shook her head vigorously, crossed out each incorrect word, and tried again. If she gave up that easily, it would only make things harder moving forward. Not to mention that she'd have to learn to speak again from scratch, a daunting task for anyone, much less someone who'd prided herself on being articulate and expressive throughout her life.

How am I going to tell everyone what's happened? Karin agonized. *What if I can never talk or write again?*

The following day, confined to her hospital bed, Karin received a visit from her friends Abby and Robert Redmond. Robert had an idea.

"If it's okay with you, I'd like to start a Facebook group called 'Feel Better Karin,'" he said, sensing his friend's uncharacteristic frustration. "We'll invite as many people as we can, and it'll be a way for us to keep everyone up-to-date on your progress."

Karin was already a member of Facebook and thought Robert's plan sounded like a good one. Maybe she'd even be able to take over once she could type again. She nodded in agreement. Before long, Robert had designed the page, with a photo of Karin and a description that read:

Karin, our good friend and accomplished triathlete, on Sunday, February 8th, suffered a mild stroke. She is now in recovery and is getting stronger and better with every moment.

While we've received Karin's blessing to create this group, we don't feel we should disclose her full diagnosis—so we'll leave that to her—but know that she is safe and improving, and certain to be back online and responding to all your notes when she's able.

We've decided to create a group to 1) keep all of you informed, and 2) provide an easy space to send her a message of well wishes and warm thoughts.

And that's exactly what people did. Within days, the group had grown to 115 members—including strangers—all professing their unconditional love and support. Even Karin's father—a physician in Sweden, who'd offered to take his daughter home with him to recover—was so overwhelmed by the outpouring on Facebook and the devotion of her extensive network of friends, that he agreed it was in Karin's best interest to stay put.

Each day, her visitors would read aloud from Facebook, sharing excerpts from Karin's group page. This lifted Karin's spirits and helped motivate her to regain her strength and communication capabilities.

On the following Thursday, Karin was finally released from the hospital, and even though her father had to return home to Sweden the next day, her friends remained stalwart by her side, staying in her apartment with her to avoid possible disaster—which is exactly what happened.

On Valentine's Day, Karin experienced a transient ischemic attack (TIA), sending her back to the hospital once again. Robert's post on the "Feel Better Karin" Facebook group read:

Karin has gone back to the hospital. Anja and Abby were with her this evening at the laundromat when she began having some odd symptoms. They dialed 911 and got her back to the hospital quickly.

We'll update everyone via the group as soon as we know anything more. She is alert and speaking (a little).

From what we know at this point she is fine, but they are monitoring her.
I hope each and every one of you has a warm and happy evening. Send good vibes her way . . .

Predictably, Karin's many supporters rallied around her. And, again, her Facebook page kept her cheerful and allowed her to strategize her recuperation.

By May 1, Karin—the consummate fighter—was back at work, with her motor skills entirely restored and her speech skills not far behind. While she didn't have quite as much energy as she'd once had, she was counting on nothing less than 100 percent recovery.

These days, Karin is running and swimming again—with a snorkel. She found a group called "Carotid Artery Dissection" on Facebook, which she says has been invaluable in connecting her with other young and fit people who've endured the same thing as she did.

She expounds, "Throughout this whole ordeal, in various ways, Facebook has fostered such a huge support system for me. And I could never have gotten through this without that support. I feel so lucky to be alive and well."

But Karin wouldn't be Karin if she settled for content. In July 2010, you may just find her at the starting line for the Ironman Triathlon. "Watch me do it!" she declares. "And if for some reason I can't, it'll be the year after that. I'm not giving up on this."

TWENTY-TWO

AD *Placement*

*E*ric Barker was the ideal job applicant. Not only had he graduated a year early from the University of Pennsylvania and received a master's degree from UCLA, but he'd also gone on to realize ten successful years as a Hollywood screenwriter, his résumé a veritable list of top studios, from Disney to Twentieth Century Fox.

But after a decade spent in the notoriously cutthroat world of entertainment, the former Ivy Leaguer was ready for a change. Tired of working alone—the province of a freelancer—Eric considered his next move. He wasn't looking to abandon the media industry altogether, and, with that in mind, decided that the management end of things might prove to be a better fit. He could remain in the same field, yet in a different capacity, and, at the same time, be able to interact with other people. Of course, he'd have to get his MBA.

In the fall of 2007, Eric enrolled in Boston College's Wallace E. Carroll Graduate School of Management, as determined as ever to fulfill his professional goals. He was well aware that his ironic turn—a Hollywood screenwriter pursuing a business degree—was more like the premise for a comedy script than a true-to-life experience, but that didn't stop him from keeping his eye on the prize.

Before long, Eric was carrying a full class load of finance, statistics, and accounting—a significant leap for the undergrad philosophy major, who hadn't even taken college calculus. Sure, he'd been a Hollywood sensation, had rubbed elbows with celebrities and other bold-faced names, but in business school, no one seemed to care about his star-studded past. Eric had gone from being the guy everyone wanted to talk to at a cocktail party to a virtual nobody—practically overnight. And it didn't feel good.

Still, though, he pressed on, unwilling to let his outsider status defeat him, and that summer he was offered a coveted internship at Nintendo—the ideal outlet for amalgamating his old and new skill sets. Eric's dream was finally unfolding. His internship, as they typically did, would translate into a job post-graduation, and everything would materialize exactly as he'd planned.

Or not. As it turned out, Nintendo didn't have enduring programs that suited Eric's qualifications, and while he performed exceptionally during his time there, there had been no real plan to hire him for the long term.

Come September, Eric was right back where he'd started two months earlier, with one exception: Most of his classmates had already lined up jobs and were content to kick back and relax straight through the academic year. More to the point, the country's recession was intensifying with each passing day, rendering it increasingly difficult to secure employment. While his peers were relishing their "hired" status, Eric was making uncomfortable jokes to the effect of: "Maybe I'll stick around and get my PhD." Searching the Internet one afternoon, frantically seeking out job opportunities, Eric came across Willy Franzen's website—www.onedayonejob.com.

Willy, a fellow Ivy Leaguer who in May of 2007 had founded One Day, One Job—the insider's guide to unique and exciting entry-level job and career opportunities for recent college graduates—had set forth an intriguing idea.

He'd been using the Facebook Ads platform for about a year, starting out by targeting accomplished college seniors with ads and inviting them to check out his site for relevant information. He'd continued to run and tweak his campaign through July 2008, when he'd come across a Visa Small Business Network offer for a complimentary $100 advertising credit. Along with this credit, he'd found a few coupon codes, which had allowed him to explore the Facebook Ads Platform at no cost. At the same time, he'd been attempting to come up with new ways to reach both potential advertisers and journalists, and had begun experimenting with reaching Facebook networks that might include these journalists, or even human resources recruiters. While these campaigns hadn't achieved Willy's desired results, they *had* facilitated the realization that the Facebook Ads platform was powerful, and, additionally, had sparked a breakthrough idea.

On July 18, 2008, Willy had posted the following on his One Day, One Job website:

A couple weeks ago we came up with an off-the-wall job search idea that we want to test. Since we're not job searching ourselves, we're looking for 10 volunteers who would like to be part of an experiment. This idea is pretty "out there," but we think that it has the potential to be extremely effective. Participation will require a small time commitment (maybe an hour or two), but should be well worth it. We'll be helping and coaching you along the way to ensure that you make the most out of our idea.

AD *Placement*

To participate you must:

- *Be adventurous and up for anything.*
- *Want to start a job in the next few months (no rising college seniors).*
- *Have a clear idea of what companies you'd like to work for or at the very least what industries you'd like to work in.*
- *Keep the details of the experiment confidential while it's going on.*
- *Be willing to have your name published here on One Day, One Job and possibly on other sites or in print publications.*
- *Agree to write a short summary of the results of the experiment to be published in a future blog post.*
- *Have a Facebook account.*

We're doing this because we want to constantly push the limits of using the Internet to find and get entry-level jobs. Not only are we hoping to help participants land their dream jobs, but we're also hoping that this idea/experiment will yield valuable information for other job seekers. We even think that this idea might be innovative enough to generate some major press attention for us and the participants. Attention is a good thing when you're job searching, so sign up now!

Willy had then e-mailed those interested, explaining his idea further:

FACEBOOK *Fairytales*

Facebook allows you to target your ads very specifically. We target seniors at specific colleges with our ads, and more and more employers are trying to leverage Facebook to find great entry-level talent, but not many are doing a good job. I recently came up with the idea of reversing the roles. Instead of helping employers target students with recruitment messages, why not help students/new grads target employers with Facebook ads?

Basically, we want you to create an ad for yourself. The goal is to sell yourself in a few short sentences and convince any recruiters who may see your ads to click through to your résumé / Web page / contact information. You'll need to put together an image (a picture of you, or something that tells employers why they should hire you), a pitch about yourself in as few words as possible, and somewhere to link to. Most importantly you need a target. This will probably eliminate some of you from the experiment, but it's absolutely necessary to make the method worthwhile. Your target can be based on keywords, location, or a company. Targeting by company is the most likely to succeed, because you can guarantee that you're actually reaching people who work at companies that might consider hiring you.

You're probably saying, "but doesn't Facebook advertising cost money?" Yes, it does. Luckily, there are some current Facebook promotions that give away free advertising credits. We're planning on having you use those, although we hope you think this idea is cool enough that you'd pay for the ads if there weren't any promotions (they're pretty cheap).

AD *Placement*

Eric was intrigued. Granted, the experiment had already taken place, but the idea was still brilliant. Digging deeper, though, Eric noticed that Willy's five participants hadn't realized stellar results, and, beyond that fact, he also knew that recruitment of MBA students traditionally didn't take place until January. So he bookmarked the page, rationalizing that it might just be a crazy-enough concept to work for somebody, and why couldn't that somebody be him?

Four months later, ushering in the New Year, Eric embarked on the job hunt once again, but, by April, he'd had no success. It was the same old story every time. He'd be called in for an interview. "We're looking for someone creative, with an original mind," they'd profess. But, ultimately, they'd hire someone with a strict financial background and Eric would fall to the wayside.

Unable to garner the attention he felt he deserved, Eric revisited Willy's website. Perhaps the idea was a little "out there," but desperate times called for desperate measures, and he thought it might be just wild enough to actually work.

Without hesitation, Eric logged on to Facebook and followed Willy's instructions—which he'd since posted for public perusal—to the letter, targeting five major companies renowned for creativity, entertainment savvy, and business know-how: Microsoft, Apple, Netflix, YouTube, and IDEO (a design and innovation consultancy based in Palo Alto, California).

Eric was amazed at how simple and focused the process was. He could target people over eighteen years old or people in specific regions or zip codes. And that's exactly what he did—narrowing his concentration to current employees of his top five companies, within the United States. He was even able to exclude people whose profiles featured his keywords, despite them not working for one of the companies.

Sitting on his couch, staring at his computer screen, Eric's finger hovered over the submit button. *Would his approach be considered gauche? Would be be laughed all the way to the back of the unemployment line?* His mind brimmed with self-doubt, but his finger did the walking, and, just like that, his Facebook ad was released into the social networking universe.

A few minutes later, Eric punched the refresh key with one eye open. And boom! His ad had already received a number of hits. Over the course of the next few hours the numbers began to grow exponentially.

Days later, though, his in-box was still empty. *Did I do something wrong?* he mused. *Should I change my ad? Am I insane to have done this in the first place?*

A couple more days passed, and finally, a message appeared in Eric's in-box:

 I saw your ad on Facebook. I might be able to assist in getting your résumé to someone at Microsoft.

AD *Placement*

Eric felt like he'd won the lottery! There was a stranger out there in the vast world of cyberspace who was willing to help him find a job. And that was just the beginning. During the next few weeks, similar messages flooded Eric's in-box. Even if people weren't in a place to hire him, they were interested in what he was doing. Yet he still couldn't turn his overwhelming response into gainful employment.

Around the same time, Eric received a note from a recruiter who said he'd clicked on Eric's Facebook ad, and also, that he used to work for Microsoft. As it turned out, the recruiter also had a blog, where he posted the following about Eric:

There's this guy doing Facebook ads to find a job; isn't that cool?!

And with that, Eric saw the light. His ads may have been reaching his target companies, but what the public really hungered for was an amazing Facebook success story. Realizing the potential of his tale, Eric turned his efforts to public relations, contacting various media outlets and blogs, and sending a staggering one hundred e-mails to his vast web of contacts.

At first, he heard nothing. *Clearly, this isn't going to work out,* he finally admitted to himself. But then, in late May, Eric fielded another e-mail, this time from a friend, who was forwarding him the link to an article about his Facebook ad in the Consumerist, a well-known consumer affairs blog—an article Eric hadn't even been interviewed for, and one that subsequently saw over 23,000 page views!

Hastily, Eric plugged his name into an online search and was astounded by the results. People were writing about him, blogging about him, and just talking about him in general. They were impressed by his "out-of-the-box" idea, and, more importantly, his tireless pursuit of it. He'd taken Willy's brainchild and run with it, and his efforts were finally paying off.

Knowing he had to strike while the iron was hot, Eric immediately forwarded the Consumerist link to all of his top contacts. Before long, people were referring him for job opportunities at warp speed.

In June of 2009, roughly six weeks after placing his original Facebook ad and one month after graduating with his MBA, Eric received the e-mail he'd been waiting so long for—from a Microsoft recruiter. A forty-five-minute interview later and Eric was well on his way to joining the ranks of one of the most successful corporations in the world.

"I'm going to seek a place for you here within Microsoft," his interviewer told him.

As Eric awaits the arrival of his golden ticket, his options are ever expanding. George Lucas's company has called, as have Amazon.com and IDEO. His story has been covered by the *Boston Globe* and the *Baltimore Sun*, to name a few. Of course, he also has a whole new set of Facebook friends.

"Facebook is a community. It's all about people connecting. And, in a way, this was an experiment about people's attitudes," Eric says, reflecting on his accomplishments. "People feel good on Facebook because, in a virtual and digital sense, they're with their friends. And that carries over, I believe, into wanting to help people. If you don't believe in people, this experiment wouldn't be for you. But I can tell you one thing—if I hadn't remained optimistic about the generosity of the human spirit and confident in people's good natures, I wouldn't have the opportunities I do today."

TWENTY-THREE

HEAVEN *Sent*

On September 23, 1992, Talbot and Michelle Elkins welcomed their second daughter, Jessica, into the world, and the couple from Athens, Alabama—along with two-year-old sister, Emilee—was overjoyed. Four years later, baby brother Michael joined the family fold.

The Elkinses considered themselves the luckiest parents on Earth, with three happy and healthy children in their brood. And as the years passed, with Jessica and Emilee developing into extraordinary young ladies, life only got better.

By fifteen, Jessica was the consummate "perfect teenager," a veritable oxymoron in and of itself. She'd had a steady boyfriend for over two years, who her parents adored, and she was involved in an array of activities, ranging from ballet and jazz to gymnastics, volleyball, and, ultimately, cheerleading—her true passion. Jessica boasted an extensive group of close friends, and was revered by anyone who came to know her, as was evidenced by the 200-plus students who had voted her Homecoming representative for both her seventh- and eighth-grade school years.

At home, she acted as a second caregiver to her family, changing her brother's diapers and feeding him from the day he was born, and generally doing everything she could to help her parents, who worked full-time in their family trucking business.

Unlike many adolescent girls, Jessica was also exceptionally close to her mother, whom she'd offered to drive anywhere she'd needed to go from the day she'd received her learner's permit. The two were inseparable. So, on Thursday, December 20, when they embarked on a last-minute holiday shopping spree, it was like any other day for the Elkins gals.

They hopped from store to store, eventually seeking out a special Pandora ring that Emilee had requested at a jewelry shop in Athens. By the day's end, Michelle was eager to get home to finish up some chores before some minor post-Christmas surgery she'd scheduled for the following week.

"We have to hurry so I can get the laundry done and clean the house," she said to Jessica. "We've got a lot of things going on before my operation."

"Mom, it's not like somebody's going to die if this stuff doesn't get done," Jessica said, looking her in the eyes and smiling brightly. "The laundry will be taken care of. I promise. You don't need to worry about the little things."

Michelle laughed. After all, her middle child was wise beyond her years. *How many mothers could rely on their teenage daughter to hold down the fort so capably?* she thought, beaming with pride.

The following morning, while Michelle tied up loose ends at work, Jessica headed to school for the last of her final exams, and that afternoon joined Emilee and her boyfriend at a local Mexican eatery. Jessica couldn't have been more at ease; school was out for the Christmas holiday, and she was elated to be spending the afternoon with Emilee, who was not only her sister, but her best friend.

Midway through lunch, though, Jessica's celebratory feast took a turn for the worse. She announced, "I'm not feeling so well. I'm going to sit in the car until you're done."

"Are you sure you're okay?" her sister asked, concerned. "Go rest, and we'll be there soon."

FACEBOOK *Fairytales*

Emilee dialed her mother immediately. "Jessica is sick. She just left the table and went to sit in the car."

"Hurry and get through eating, and go check on her," Michelle urged.

"Sure thing, Mom. I'm sure she's going to be okay."

But by 1:30, back at the car, Emilee wasn't so sure anymore. She called Michelle again, somewhat frantic. "Mom, Jessica is crying a lot. She says she's aching all over."

"Let me finish what I'm doing here. Take her to the house, and I'll be there as fast as I can," Michelle instructed, hurriedly attending to her outstanding tasks.

An hour later, Michelle was home at Jessica's side, where she lay in bed, overcome with pain.

"Listen, sweetie, we're going to take you to the doctor and see what's wrong," she soothed, stroking her daughter's forehead. It was the Friday afternoon before a holiday weekend, and Michelle knew that most private practices would soon be closed.

As Jessica continued to weep, Michelle drove her to the closest physician's office, not more than three minutes away. Much to their dismay, however, when they arrived, there was a note on the door:

We are not taking any more patients for the day.

"I'm calling your pediatrician," Michelle said, helping Jessica back to the car for their twenty-minute drive to Decatur.

She probably has the flu, Michelle told herself. *There's nothing serious to worry about.* Still, her maternal instinct was telling her to make sure.

At the pediatrician's office, Michelle sat next to her daughter as she was prodded and probed. Jessica was given a throat culture, which made her sick to her stomach, and a flu test, the result of which was positive. Michelle's relief was tangible. The flu was no fun, but it was certainly manageable.

With the doctor's recommendation of "liquids and plenty of rest," and a prescription for Tamiflu in hand, they drove home to put Jessica back in bed, where she'd recuperate for the next few days.

But things didn't go exactly as planned. Jessica continued to vomit routinely, and Michelle and Talbot were worried that their daughter wasn't ingesting the medicine she needed to get better. They also feared that she would become severely dehydrated.

Michelle called the doctor to explain the situation.

"Don't give her anything else by mouth—no water, nothing," the pediatrician on call advised. "Just try to get her through the night and keep her as calm as you can. The flu has to run its course. You're in for a rough couple of days."

Michelle was comforted again. *We'll just watch her closely through the night and keep her siblings out of the room, so they don't contract this too,* she reasoned.

And that's just what they did. Talbot checked on his daughter every few hours, and, by Saturday morning, it seemed that Jessica was doing a little better.

Michelle quietly went about her ironing, continuing to tackle the household duties she fretted would accumulate while she was in the hospital for her surgery. She knew Jessica would do whatever she could to assist, but she didn't want her to have to, especially when she'd be recovering from a bad bout of the flu.

"Mom! Mom!" Jessica's voice interrupted the silence.

"I'm coming, baby. I'm on my way." Michelle called out, rushing to her ailing daughter's room to find her sick to her stomach yet again. "Let's get you back into bed," she said once the vomiting had ceased. "You're going to feel better real soon."

As she helped Jessica—wearing only a short nightshirt and underwear—roll onto her side, Michelle spotted a quarter-sized bruise on the side of her hip.

"Jess, did you run into something and hurt your hip? How did you get this bruise?" she asked, motioning to the mark.

"Mom, I haven't done anything. I don't know how I got it," she replied faintly.

Michelle began to examine her body. There were small purple spots everywhere. "I'll be right back, baby. I'm going to call Daddy."

Hastily, she dialed Talbot, who'd run into work to pick up a FedEx package—a special gift for Jessica's boyfriend that had arrived at the last minute. "There's something more going on with Jessica than the flu. Hurry home."

Within the hour, Talbot and Michelle were rushing their daughter to the hospital while she fell in and out of consciousness in the backseat. Forty-five minutes later, in the emergency room, the doctor finally arrived, checked Jessica's vitals, and asked a series of questions. The doctor then stepped out of the room to confer with a colleague, and when he returned twenty minutes later—wearing gloves and a mask—he had tears in his eyes.

"We're going to have to move her to a children's hospital in Birmingham," he said.

"That's two hours away!" Michelle was troubled.

"We're almost certain that she has meningitis. We're starting her on the strongest antibiotics we have to help her fight this. Anybody that's been around her also has to go on antibiotics." His voice cracked. "Mr. and Mrs. Elkins, your daughter is very sick. Sometimes kids don't pull through this."

Michelle began sobbing as Talbot comforted her in his embrace.

"We're going to do everything we can to save her."

Paralyzed with shock and pain, Michelle and Talbot drove the two hours to Birmingham, while Jessica was transported by helicopter. Once they'd arrived, the nurse handed Michelle her daughter's ring.

"We had to take off all her jewelry, so you hold on to this," she said, offering a sympathetic pat on the arm.

Michelle slipped the ring onto her finger and began to cry. *What was going on? Jessica had the flu. Just the flu. Not meningitis. Not something that could take their sweet baby away.*

By the Sunday before Christmas, in the Intensive Care Unit, Jessica was diagnosed with pneumonia, and as her condition worsened, doctors were forced to insert a breathing tube down her throat, in order to give her lungs a chance to rest.

The following day, her kidneys began to fail, and it became clear that they could very well shut down altogether.

As Michelle and Talbot rode the roller coaster that had become their life—and the life of their fifteen-year-old daughter—they tried desperately to hold on to their faith.

On Christmas Day, the Elkinses' immediate and extended families gathered at the hospital for lunch. Michelle wept inconsolably, terrified that her daughter might not live to see her sixteenth birthday.

Later that afternoon, the Elkinses listened intently as a dozen hospital staffers discussed Jessica's fate—how they could wean her off the breathing tube, if they could wean her off it at all.

"It's going to be a long process," the doctor said, furrowing his brow.

A long process we can deal with—just don't let her leave us, Michelle prayed, leaning down to stroke her daughter's ice-cold face and warm her frozen appendages. She was all too aware that one of the consequences of meningitis was a loss of limbs. But that was the least of her worries. All she wanted—needed—was for her precious baby girl to endure.

Minutes later, though, Jessica's blood pressure began to spike, shooting up and down like a yo-yo, and, all of a sudden, there was little movement in her once-vibrant eyes. The doctors hurried in, asking Michelle and Talbot to remain outside for what seemed like the longest and most agonizing wait of their lives.

"She's started suffering mini strokes," the doctor finally reported. "The left side of her brain has been severely damaged." As Talbot and Michelle processed this heartbreaking news, Jessica continued to experience more strokes, leaving her brain entirely inactive.

Over the course of the next twenty-four hours, 400 of Jessica's friends gathered at the hospital to bid farewell to the "perfect teenager" they'd once loved and admired.

And, by the afternoon of December 26, 2007, Talbot and Michelle had turned their beloved child over to the arms of God, where they believe she'll spend eternity, safe and happy.

The grieving process that followed was fraught with pain and anguish for the entire Elkins clan. The members of their community and beyond rallied around them with unconditional support. Jessica's friends designed a T-shirt in her honor, to raise money for meningitis awareness. Their friends donated money to ease the burden of medical expenses, and organized a walk that brought in over $10,000. There were also two college scholarships formed in Jessica's name.

Perhaps the most touching acknowledgment of all, though, was when the city of Athens, Alabama, declared September 23, Jessica's birthday, "Meningitis Awareness Day."

Despite the outpouring of support, Michelle and Talbot needed to find their own ways to mourn their unthinkable loss. Michelle began attending meningitis conferences and championing her new cause as a means of managing her heartache. She knew Jessica would want her to help save the lives of others. Talbot took a different approach. He turned to Facebook, the social networking site his daughter had been entranced by, and—with the help of his brother, Keith—started a Facebook group called "In Memory of Jessica Elkins."

Within the first six days, the group had attracted over 1,000 members. Encouraged, they also designed a "cause page," which read:

 This is a public awareness site to urge parents to vaccinate their children in memory of 15-year-old Jessica Elkins, of Athens, Alabama, who died of bacterial meningitis on December 26, 2007. The purpose of this

cause is to help spread the word about the
dangers of meningitis and to educate parents
on available vaccines that may help save their
child.

Overseeing both groups became a coping mechanism
for Talbot, who, today, provides updates to nearly 6,000
members, collectively, across the globe.

What's helped him the most, however, has been
the practice of sending daily Facebook messages to his
daughter—even though the messages will never be
answered—and to communicate, as well, via Facebook
with her many friends.

"I've been writing Facebook notes to my daughter
every day for two years," Talbot confides. "And I'll never
stop. It's my way of keeping our connection alive and
maintaining my faith."

Michelle, who's now a Facebook member as well, and,
to this day, wears Jessica's ring, recounts the tender tale that
has, in part, allowed her to persevere: "A few years ago,
Jessica attended a church function with her youth group.
Recently, I found out that on that trip, while chatting with
friends, my beautiful daughter spoke these words: 'I just
can't wait to get to heaven—to see what it's like there.'"

Michelle pauses, smiling wistfully. "All this time, I've
known where she is, and how she is, but to know she
couldn't wait to get there has afforded me a true sense of
peace."

TWENTY-FOUR

ACROSS AN *Ocean*

$\mathcal{I}$t may have taken place on April Fools' Day, but there was nothing funny about it.

Russell Alton,[*] a sixteen-year-old Oxfordshire boy, logged on to his Facebook page and scanned his list of friends to see who he might connect with.

It was an unseasonably cold night in southeast England, with temperatures well below freezing, and the chill in the air wasn't solely outside.

Things hadn't been going well for Russell. Well beyond the typical teenage angst, he felt miserable and depressed, and—above all—desperate to escape his relentless despair. Searching for a friendly face, he settled on a teenage girl in Maryland named Rachel Parker.* So what if she was on the other side of the Atlantic Ocean? They were both on Facebook—the ultimate geographical equalizer—which made it possible to chat with anyone across the globe at any hour, despite being in different time zones. Perhaps he thought she'd offer a sympathetic ear. Or perhaps, he reasoned, she'd be too far away to do anything. After all, they were virtual strangers who had somehow connected via the popular social networking site.

Russell inhaled deeply, typed his private message to Rachel, and pressed send:

I'm going to take a drug overdose. I intend to commit suicide.

The menacing words appeared on Rachel's screen and her body stiffened with fear, while her mind filled with questions. *Was this some kind of joke? Why would he tell me? Should I do something about it? Or will I be wasting people's time on nothing more than an April Fools' prank?*

Rachel couldn't let it go. What if he was reaching out to her because he didn't have anyone else to turn to? She definitely had to do something. But what?

Without further hesitation, she called her mother into the room and motioned to her screen, displaying the mysterious message.

"I barely even know this boy, and I have no idea exactly where he lives," she explained. "What should we do?"

Her mother's face flooded with alarm. "We need to report this to the authorities. Suicide threats cannot be taken lightly," she insisted, and promptly contacted the local Maryland police department.

"My daughter received a suicide threat from one of her Facebook friends—a sixteen-year-old boy in England," she conveyed to the officer on the other end of the line. "We have no way of knowing if it's real, but we thought we should alert you."

Maryland Police, agreeing that the threat was worthy of urgent attention, called a "special agent" at the White House, who, in turn, contacted the British Embassy in Washington, D.C. Ultimately, by early Thursday morning, news of Russell's message had reached the Thames Valley Police Department, on the north side of the River Thames in south Oxfordshire.

Police commander chief superintendent Brendan O'Dowda fielded the call, and with the nebulous information in hand, worked industriously—along with his staff—searching the electoral roll websites to narrow down the boy's location to eight potential addresses. Still unaware as to whether the tale was true, O'Dowda dispatched officers to each of the eight locations, and, by the fourth home, they had their answer. Russell was in bad shape, but still conscious.

Having overdosed on drugs, just as his message to Rachel had said, Russell was rushed by ambulance to the John Radcliffe Hospital in Oxford, where, through specialized treatment, he made a full recovery.

"It would have been quite easy for any number of people to decide there wasn't enough information," reflects Chief Superintendent O'Dowda. "But due to the tenacity and professionalism of those people, we managed to pin down eight addresses, then went through the painful and laborious process of visiting each of them in order to find the lad. It took up time and effort, but it was time and effort absolutely well spent."

* *Names have been changed to protect the privacy of the individuals involved.*
** *Adapted from articles on: www.thesun.co.uk and http://news.bbc.co.uk. Quotes are not direct and are based on information provided by these sources.*

TWENTY-FIVE

SUMMER *Love*

The year was 1984. Ronald Reagan was in the White House. Tina Turner and Bruce Springsteen were topping the charts. And the price of a movie ticket was two dollars and fifty cents. The setting was Camp Avnet in Long Beach, New York.

Roni Tropper, a petite fifteen-year-old with an olive complexion, layered eighties bangs, and dark eyebrows framing her deep chocolate eyes, smiled across the dining hall at Allen Applbaum, a dangerously cute sixteen-and-a-half-year-old, whom she'd had a crush on since the beginning of the summer.

He smiled back. After all, Allen held a torch for Roni too, even though he was dating another camper—a girl Roni had just become friends with.

Roni and Allen often hung out together in large groups, and as the summer drew to a close, they promised to keep in touch with each other. Roni's bubbly personality was contagious, and Allen wanted to be around her as often as possible. And she, in turn, was drawn to his charm. But, as often happens with camp camaraderie, even though they lived in neighboring towns on Long Island, their reunions were few. Before long, Roni and Allen lost touch and went their separate ways.

Fast-forward three years, to Roni's first day of classes at City University of New York in Queens. A new student with no friends to speak of, she scanned the crowded cafeteria for an empty seat. What she found instead was a familiar face. Standing directly in her line of vision was Allen!

"I can't believe this!" Roni exclaimed.

"It's so great to see you again!" Allen smiled.

Small talk was followed by an intense catch-up lunch, and soon, Roni and Allen had forged a renewed friendship that centered on daily carpooling to and from school. As it happened, Roni's parents were overly protective; although she'd recently gotten her driver's license, they were unwilling to let her brave the few miles to school. So Allen picked her up every morning and dropped her off at home at the end of each day in his beat-up, old gray car. He even helped her hone her driving skills.

One day Allen's car died in Roni's parents' driveway. "You'll have to drive your car today," he said. "We have to get to class. I have a test."

Roni was worried, as her parents didn't allow her to drive much farther than the local theater and shops, but with Allen's encouragement and his pending exam, she made it all the way. From that day forward, Roni was allowed to drive on her own, and she and Allen took turns at the wheel.

It may sound like a fairytale ending, but there was one glitch. Again, Allen had a girlfriend. He'd been in a relationship for some time, and, regardless of his lingering feelings for Roni, he didn't think it would be right to act on them. But that doesn't mean he didn't want to.

Day after day, Allen would wait for Roni in the school cafeteria and would sulk silently as she flitted around the room, talking to everyone but him. When she finally did land in his vicinity, she'd be off and buzzing around again before he knew it. And while he couldn't pinpoint the feeling at the time, what he had was a serious case of jealousy. He wanted Roni all to himself.

On one particular afternoon, Allen and Roni were sitting in her bedroom after school, talking about nothing important, when he decided he desperately wanted to kiss her. But before he could muster the courage, the moment had passed.

For Roni's part, she didn't know how Allen truly felt because of his romantic reserve. She still had a crush on him as well, but had no idea that he was feeling the same way. And, once again, the pair fell victim to bad timing. Allen ended up transferring from Queens College after a year, and the two lost touch.

What had seemed like a case of destiny intervening never materialized, and while Allen eventually spent nine years in Georgia with his wife and son, Roni moved around the country—from New York to New Mexico to Texas, and ultimately, to Arizona, where she lived for thirteen years.

They no longer had any mutual friends, and Roni's family had relocated to Arizona to be closer to her. It looked as though Roni and Allen would never see each other again.

If not for Facebook, they probably never would have.

On September 24, 2008—in the middle of what felt like the longest work week ever—Roni sat at her desk in her law office, sluggishly pushing through paperwork, until a message cut through the monotony. Twenty-four years after that fateful summer at Camp Avnet, Allen had sent Roni a friend request on Facebook with the smallest hope that it would finally be their time.

Roni was elated to find Allen's name in her in-box. She couldn't help but hope that he was single. And he was. Allen was now back in New York after splitting up with his wife. Roni and Allen exchanged flirtatious notes on Facebook throughout the day, as if no time had passed since they were teenagers. During their first phone conversation, Roni admitted, "You know, I owe you a big thank-you. If not for you, I'd still only be allowed to drive within a five-mile radius of my parents' house!"

Two months later, after a whirlwind online romance, Allen flew west to visit Roni for a week. It was, as always, a swelteringly hot and sunny day in Arizona, and as Roni waited anxiously in the air-conditioned airport terminal, she was worried she might not recognize Allen after all those years. *What if he wasn't as cute as the photo he'd sent?* But when she saw him passing through the gate, she was far from disappointed. Allen ran toward her, dropped his bag, and kissed her.

"I should have done that about two decades ago," exclaimed Allen, overcome by joy.

Thrilled and relieved that all of the same feelings were still there, Roni and Allen savored their short time together. Allen met all of her friends, who'd heard more than their fair share about him, and agreed wholeheartedly that the pair was destined to be together. Perhaps the biggest highlight for Roni was when she reintroduced Allen to her parents over dinner.

When the week was over, it became obvious that, with Allen heading back to his life in New York, things were not destined to be as idyllic as they'd have liked. Allen wasn't convinced that a long-distance relationship could work, nor did he think moving would be an option, because of his fifteen-year-old son. Also, Roni didn't want to go back to New York. Her life was in Arizona. Her father's health wasn't great—he'd had a triple bypass in 2001—so being close to him was a must.

Frustrated, to say the least, Roni and Allen couldn't believe their good fortune in being reunited, but, at the same time, their misfortune that it may not work out, yet again. But they both knew one thing for sure: They absolutely couldn't let each other go.

Back in New York, Allen was heartbroken. Going about his daily routine—living in Queens and commuting to Manhattan for work—he felt sad all the time. Nothing in his life seemed right without the missing ingredient—Roni.

Desperate to alleviate his grief, Allen said to himself: *It's now or never. I need to take a leap of faith.* He decided he'd move cross-country to be with Roni. His son was old enough to visit frequently, he reasoned, and would certainly enjoy a sunny respite from chilly East Coast winters. Things were finally looking up, and Allen couldn't wait to share his news with Roni.

Then an unexpected tragedy struck—one that Roni was sure would be the final straw in separating the lovebirds for good. It was November 21, and Allen and Roni were enjoying their daily morning phone call on her way to work when her mother beeped through. Screaming and crying, her jumbled words came across the line: "The dog is bleeding on the floor! I've called 911!" And then the phone went dead.

Roni immediately told Allen she'd have to call him back so that she could tell her mother to cancel 911. As a longtime animal lover, Roni knew the emergency service wouldn't dispatch for a pet. But when she finally got ahold of her mother again, Roni found out she'd misunderstood. It wasn't the dog; it was her father. His brain had hemorrhaged.

Like Roni and Allen, Roni's parents had met when they were teenagers. Sadly, her father passed away two days before their forty-seventh wedding anniversary.

Naturally, Allen got on the first plane to Arizona and stayed for ten days, taking care of Roni and her family—running back and forth to Roni's nearby home to look after Franky and Roxy, her one- and-two-year-old shar-peis, so that she didn't have to leave her mother's side.

Ultimately, though, Allen had to return to New York, and Roni was left in a state of despair.

Perpetually crying and uncharacteristically depressed, Roni couldn't function in her everyday life, much less in a new relationship. Allen struggled with being thousands of miles away and unable to comfort his girlfriend. Although Allen hadn't known Roni's father well, he knew that he'd been a very important part of Roni's life, and it tore him apart to be away from her during her darkest hour. He still wanted to move to Arizona, but he knew Roni wouldn't be able to think along those lines—not yet, at least. She wanted to devote all of her energy to her mother and didn't think she'd have any time left for Allen. Against every instinct she had, Roni called Allen and said, "Let's call it off. My life took a bad turn. I don't know what I can offer you anymore."

December came and went, and the two continued to communicate via Facebook. Roni no longer had time for long phone conversations, as any spare moments she had were spent with her mother. This was particularly difficult for Allen, who felt the loss of not hearing her voice every day. But despite all these obstacles, Allen and Roni still couldn't let each other go.

"The only way to give our relationship a fair shot, after all these years, is for me to move west so we can be together full-time," Allen finally said.

Roni agreed.

And on January 9, 2009, he headed to Arizona for the third time in three months.

During his first visit, Allen and Roni had taken lots of photos, but the chip in Allen's camera had been corrupted, so they had been deleted. During Allen's second visit, for Roni's father's passing, the mood hadn't been conducive to posing for snapshots. So, left with no glossy pics to commemorate their times together, Allen asked innocently, "Can we please take some photos together?" Roni complied.

Sitting on Allen's lap, comforted by his strong arms cinching her waist, Roni smiled for the camera while Allen plotted his next move.

Turning to her, with one fist clenched, he unfolded his fingers slowly to reveal a small, black velvet box. Roni's eyes widened and her mouth fell open.

"Will you marry me?" he asked, gazing at her with twenty-four years' worth of accumulated affection.

Recovering from her initial state of shock, Roni screamed, "Yes!" Together, they cried tears of happiness.

Eager to spread the exciting news, Roni and Allen rushed over to her mother's shop, Terra Rosa Fine Jewelry and Gifts, in Old Town Scottsdale. They kept mum at first, as Roni's mom complained about her usual headaches as a small business owner. All the while, Roni was swinging her left hand practically in her mother's face. When the glint of the ring finally caught her eye, she shrieked with delight, hugged her daughter and son-in-law-to-be, and led Roni into the back room.

Crying softly, Roni asked, "Mom, is it okay to be this happy so soon after Dad died?"

"Let me tell you something your father said when we were reintroduced to Allen at dinner," her mother began. "He said, 'Now I can die, because Roni is taken care of.' So, yes, it's more than okay."

Their next stop was visiting Roni's father at the cemetery. It just wouldn't feel real to her, she said, until she got to share the news with her dad.

One month later, Roni and Allen were back in the car together, this time in a U-Haul, moving Allen's belongings from New York to Arizona so they could finally have the happily-ever-after they'd waited so long for. Escaping New York just before a threatening snowstorm moved in, luck was finally on their side as the pair conquered thousands of miles, winding through dark mountains and traversing barren plains.

Having arrived safely in Arizona, in the midst of unpacking Allen's things, Roni uncovered an old box in the garage that had traveled with her from state to state through the years but had never been opened. Full of diaries and camp autograph books, Roni retrieved one and it opened right to Allen's page; they both got chills. Of course, he'd made some silly joke about her diminutive size—acknowledging the discrepancy between her four-foot-six build and his six feet.

Looking further through the book, they spotted a note from Allen's ex, the girl Allen had dated that summer at Camp Avnet. It read: *Roni, thanks so much for all your help with Allen!*

"Why did I help her? I had a crush on you!" Roni laughed aloud at the irony. "You know, I could have saved myself a lot of heartache all these years with all of those men who were so wrong for me."

Allen hugged her closely and explained, "People come in and out of your life at certain times for certain reasons. We had to experience everything we have and become the people we are today so that I can finally marry you!"

And marry her he will. With family and friends cheering them on, Roni and Allen will be united once and for all amid the picturesque Arizona landscape in the spring of 2010.

Looking back, Roni ruminates, "I've definitely dated a lot of frogs. But without this amazing modern tool—Facebook—I may never have rediscovered my prince."

Acknowledgments

$\mathcal{I}$ have to admit, I've always wanted to write an acknowledgments page, at least as much as I've wanted to write a book. It's sort of the Academy Awards acceptance speech for authors, and for those of us with little acting talent, it's the closest we'll likely come. So without further ado . . .

The very first person I need to thank is my agent, Jessica Regel. Jess, you are not only a brilliant literary mastermind, but a very patient soul and a dear friend. I can't thank you enough for having faith in me from day one, and for never allowing that faith to falter, even when mine did. You've entertained my many questions and concerns and basically just listened to me agonize day after day after day, without a rumbling of complaint. I look forward to a long career working together. Oh, and you're gorgeous and wickedly funny too (had to throw those in). Plus, who else can I talk reality TV with—*endlessly?*

Thank you, also, to Jennifer Weltz and Tara Hart at the Jean V. Naggar Literary Agency. And of course, to the agency's namesake herself—Jean V. Naggar. I like to think of you all as my second family!

Next, a very big thank-you to my editor, Julie Matysik. We did it! Julie, you too are one of the most patient people on the planet. In fact, I don't think I've ever witnessed you lose your cool. Your wise insights from day one helped shape this book into what it is today, and you did so with a smile on your face and a cheerful lilt to your voice at all times. If ever I had even a passing concern, you were always there at the other end of the phone line or returning my e-mails faster than I could send them. How do you do that? It's a talent, really.

Thank you to my publisher, Tony Lyons, who took a chance on a first-time author. I think it's going to pay off, Tony. Didn't I promise you an enormous office with

Acknowledgments

panoramic views? Fingers crossed. And I can't forget the rest of my fabulous Skyhorse team: Bill Wolfsthal, Ann Treistman, Tommy Semosh, and LeAnna Weller Smith—who's responsible for the beautiful design, inside and out. I'm so grateful for your endless reservoirs of attention.

This book would not have been possible without the AMAZING Facebook crew, who devoted way more time and energy to this project than I ever could have hoped for: Brandee Barker (Facebook goddess, whom I'm forever indebted to), Tim Kendall, Ben Barry, and Devon Corvasce at OutCast Communications, who was an invaluable help in finding some of these stories.

A spotlight thank-you to Mark Zuckerberg for taking time out of his very busy schedule to interview for the foreword. I think it goes without saying that this book would not have been possible without you. Facebook has united so many millions of people worldwide, and those connections are saving lives. What you've done is truly heroic. Thank you to Chris Hughes, as well, for not only cofounding Facebook, but also for taking the time to recount his spectacular success story of working with President Barack Obama.

Thank you to Jason Corliss, my wonderful lecture agent, for taking a chance on me and keeping me on point with your witty banter. Let's book thousands of lectures! I'm ready!

Without the following people who have supported me through the years and through the composition of this book, I would never be where I am today: Kerry Kennedy; Mariah, Cara, and Michaela Kennedy Cuomo (the little sisters I never had); Stan Pottinger; Joni Evans; Seema Boesky; Tom Yellin; Andrew Cuomo; Cristina Greeven Cuomo; Steven Brill; my best friend, Melody Lineback Drake; my dear friends Jonathan and Jodie Boies; Shari and Jason Weaver (brilliant writer and photographer, respectively); Meghann Kruming; Zoe Schaeffer; Sara Haines; Liz Karp Bitton; Jayne Chase; Jennifer Goodkind; Vanessa Wakeman; Monica Lynn; Jennifer Heitler; Jennifer Scott; Jennifer Lisman Oliver; Amy Kallesten; Lisa Lineback; Sam Zises; Robert Redmond; and Brian Puskas.

Possibly the most important people to thank are all of the brave and beautiful subjects of these stories. Thank you for your time, for your stories, and for having faith that I'd do you justice. Not only are you the glue that holds this book together, but you're also new friends, whom I will cherish for years to come.

I would not be the person I am today without the unconditional love, support, and encouragement of my parents, Tom and Kyle Einhorn, my brother Zack Einhorn, my grandmother Ailene Rickel, and my grandparents Harvey and Patricia Einhorn. I love you all more than you know. You are the ones who inspire me every day. Thank you, also, to my in-laws: Mary Ann and Peter S. Liebert and Peter B., Karren, Sara, and Alex Liebert.

I've saved the best for last . . . my boys. To my husband, Lewis Liebert: Thank you doesn't really seem to

Acknowledgments

cover it. You listened to me yammer on about this book for months on end, offered your trademark wisdom, and kept your mouth shut and smiled when you knew it was a losing battle. You are my best friend, protector, and absolute hero. I love you. Oh, and . . . thanks, sweetie!

Finally, to the light of my life, my little dumpling—Jaxsyn Alvin Liebert. Being your mommy is the most precious gift of all time.

FOR FURTHER *Information*

For more information about this book and to share and read other inspirational stories resulting from Facebook connections, please become a fan of *Facebook Fairytales* at http://www.facebook.com/FacebookFairytales.

And for more information about the author, please visit her website at www.emilyliebert.com.